Unwin Education Books

PHILOSOPHY AND HUMAN MOVEMENT

Unwin Education Books

Series Editor: Ivor Morrish, BD, BA, Dip. Ed. (London), BA (Bristol)

By the same author

Expression in Movement and the Arts (London: Lepus Books,
Henry Kimpton Publishers, 1974)

Unwin Education Books

Series Editor: Ivor Morrish

Philosophy and Human Movement

DAVID BEST, MA (Cantab.), B.Phil. (York), Ph.D. (Wales)
Department of Philosophy, University College of Swansea

London
GEORGE ALLEN & UNWIN
Boston   Sydney

GEORGE ALLEN & UNWIN LTD
40 Museum Street, London WC1A 1LU

©George Allen & Unwin (Publishers) Ltd, 1978

British Library Cataloguing in Publication Data

Best, David
    Philosophy and Human Movement – (Unwin
    education books).
    1. Human mechanics   2. Mind and body
    I. Title
    612'.76'01   QP303   78–40545

ISBN   0–04–370088–8
ISBN   0–04–370089–6 Pbk

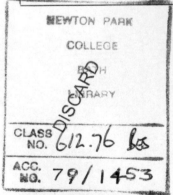
Typeset in 10 on 11 point Times by Trade Linotype Ltd
Printed in Great Britain by
Billing & Sons Ltd, Guildford, London and Worcester

Acknowledgements

It is difficult to know how to go about writing the acknowledgements for this book since so many people, especially in Britain, Canada and the USA, have been kind enough to invite me to speak on some of the relevant topics at a range of colleges and universities, as a consequence of which many stimulating points have arisen in discussion. People in these and other countries have also very kindly written to offer interesting comments on earlier and related published work. I should like to express my warm thanks to all of them.

However, there are some whom I must mention in particular.

I am very grateful indeed to many of my former colleagues of the Chelsea School of Human Movement (former Chelsea College of Physical Education, Eastbourne) for so generously and enthusiastically giving their time not only to show me and discuss the varied and interesting work they are doing, but also for offering helpful comments on early drafts of papers on some of the topics included in this book. In this respect I am particularly grateful to Hilary Corlett, and Rita Arkley, the School Librarian, who has given unstinted help in this and innumerable other ways.

I am indebted to many friends in North America for their warm interest in and support for my work. I am particularly grateful to Professor Rose Hill, of McMaster University, Ontario, for arranging on two occasions a series of seminars for faculty from various Canadian universities at which I was invited to present papers on some of the relevant issues. I should like to express my thanks to those who attended for the lively and stimulating debate which ensued.

I am also particularly indebted to Professor R. F. Atkinson, of the University of York, Dr T. J. Diffey, of the University of Sussex, Colin Phillips, of the University of Essex, and my colleague Howard Mounce, for their kindness in reading and offering helpful comments upon early drafts of articles on some of these topics. I am very grateful to Professor D. Z. Phillips, of the University College of Swansea, for the continued and generous support he has given in general for the work I am doing.

Although he has not directly contributed to this book, I cannot lose the opportunity of expressing my gratitude to Professor H. T. A. Whiting of Vrije Universiteit, Amsterdam, for the considerable help and consistent support he has so warmly offered to me since I began work in this field.

My greatest debt is owed to my colleague David Cockburn, who was generous enough to give his time to subject to rigorous critical examination the first draft of this book, to discuss at some length with me some of the problems which arose, and to make many helpful suggestions for improvement.

To
my good friends in Canada

Cover photograph of Sue Harding by Bob Gleave.

Contents

Introduction

It may be worth making clear at the outset a point discussed in a little more detail at the end of Chapter 5, that I shall use the term 'human movement' as a generic one to include human kinetics, physical education, sport and dance. I am not concerned with what seem to me rather sterile arguments about terminology. An exception is Chapter 2 where, of necessity, I have to some extent to follow the meaning of the term employed by the authors on whom I comment.

Chapters 2, 3 and 4 are revised versions of material already published in the *Journal of Human Movement Studies*. Chapter 7 is a revised and considerably extended version of material originally published in the *British Journal of Aesthetics*.

The recurrence of the body/mind problem in various forms in different chapters reflects my increasingly confirmed conviction that confusion on this complex underlying issue is the biggest single source of misconception in the literature on human movement. It has widespread and severely damaging ramifications, with respect not only to a wide range of theoretical discussion, but also to important practical issues. I draw attention to some of these at appropriate points.

I have tried to arrange the chapters according to degree of difficulty since this book is intended primarily for students with little or no background in formal philosophy. I have selected the topics for consideration which, as far as I can judge from my lecturing on both sides of the Atlantic, seem to be of greatest interest and relevance to those in the field of human movement. In some of the earlier chapters I adopt a somewhat lighthearted style, since philosophy seems to have a daunting reputation, hence it seemed worth trying to spice the logical points with a little humour. As I state in Chapter 1, my overriding aim is to encourage students to think for themselves, and to achieve this it is necessary sometimes to make my points in a provocative way. However, I hope this will not be misconstrued as a lack of respect for the authors whom I criticise. On the contrary, that they make philosophical errors does not in the least detract from the important contribution which many of them have made to progress in practical work in the field of human movement. I am well aware of the great debt which is owed to many of these authors, some of whom, for instance, have pioneered a new and valuable approach to dance, gymnastics and other forms of movement in schools. Hence I should like explicitly and firmly to disavow any intention to belittle the contribution they have made in this respect.

Chapter 1

Philosophy and Human Movement

INTRODUCTION

One of the most damaging misconceptions encountered in considering
the field of human-movement studies from a philosophical point of
view is a misconception about philosophy itself and what it can
achieve. This misconception is by no means limited to students and
faculty of the relevant departments in colleges and universities, but is
found even among some of those who have gained reputations as
philosophers of sport, physical education and dance. Hence it is
important at the outset to make as clear as possible what I take to be
the character, scope and contribution of modern philosophy. The task
is a difficult one since it is impossible to provide an answer which is
both concise and accurate to the question: 'What is philosophy?' This
is partly because the issues which engage philosophers are so varied,
and partly because there are deep divisions of opinion about the
character of the discipline. For this reason I shall concentrate predominantly on offering an outline of philosophical *method*, since this
aspect of philosophy is less contentious, and moreover it has a
particularly important contribution to make, especially at this stage in
the development of the study of human movement. There may be
details of the outline I shall give which are open to dispute, and some
oversimplification is inevitable, but I think there would be broad
agreement about it, at least in most philosophy departments of
English-speaking universities. Contention arises more over the subject
matter than over the methodology of philosophy.

MISCONCEPTIONS

One of the most prevalent misconceptions is to suppose that
philosophy consists of speculative theorising of a quasi-religious or
poetic nature, including the proposal or hypothesis of a metaphysical
system of life or world order. An example of such a conception of
philosophy can be found in Chekhov's play *The Three Sisters*. At a
certain stage of boredom in a social gathering someone suggests that
those present might like to philosophise, and this consists in stalking
earnestly to and fro speculating on what the world will be like in two
or three hundred years, and on what is the purpose of life. In much the
same vein, one speaks of, for example, Eastern or mystic philo-

sophies, which are largely religious or quasi-religious recommendations as to how one should conduct one's life. *Weltanschauung*, in German, adequately captures this conception, which is roughly equivalent to the English term 'philosophy of life'. To explain one's philosophy of life is to give an account, for instance, of one's overriding aims and principles, and what one considers to be most important. What might be called the poetic or romantic view of philosophy is related to this *Weltanschauung* sense. For example, a colleague once invited me to look at a calendar which she thought would interest me as a philosopher. She indicated the page for the current month, on which there was a short homily in the form of a poem. However, whether or not it would interest me would depend upon what I thought of it *as* a homily or poem. Such a work is unlikely to be of philosophical interest.

Similarly, what is called the 'philosophy of sport' or 'philosophy of physical education' often consists in speculative theorising purporting to provide some sort of comforting metaphysical justification for the value of the activities concerned, and for the importance of their inclusion in the school curriculum.

Another related sense of the term was introduced to me by a former American student, who spoke of what she called 'experiential philosophy'. Students at her institution were apparently urged, whenever they were performing normal, everyday activities, to be aware of everything around them. While walking along the road, for instance, they were encouraged to notice the birds singing, the wind in the trees and the clouds scudding by. Now whatever may be the merits of such an exercise, it certainly is not philosophy, at least in my sense of the term. Its relation to the misty metaphysical sense adumbrated above became apparent when she explained that later in the course there was a discussion of the philosophy of basketball. Apparently, although she had been an enthusiastic player for many years, it was, she said, only as a result of that course that she was able to understand the game's philosophy. When I expressed bewilderment about what could be meant by this, she insisted that there *must* be a philosophy of basketball, since there must be a reason why the game is played. In much the same vein, the manager of the England soccer team was asked on a television programme for his philosophy of football.

CRITICISM AND CLARIFICATION

If one had to describe them very concisely one might characterise the methods of philosophy as consisting in criticism and clarification, tracing out the logical consequences of what people say, and revealing the logical structure of language. Sometimes the result of such critical philosophical questioning can be, as Wittgenstein (1953) put it, the uncovering of disguised nonsense in order to reveal it as plain nonsense. This remark indicates one of the main contributions which philosophy can make to the study of human movement. It also suggests the important point that there is a good sense in which philosophy is not just another specialist subject. It has a relation to all academic subjects, since philosophers study the nature of all kinds of knowledge and inquiry, they reason about the nature of reasoning. In order to understand the character of philosophy one should recognise that there is a difference between doing something, and describing how it is done. For instance, the best mathematicians are not necessarily, or even usually, the best philosophers of mathematics. Bertrand Russell made one of the greatest contributions to the philosophy of mathematics, yet he was not himself a great mathematician. Similarly, Karl Popper is generally regarded as one of the greatest philosophers of science, although he is not a scientist. Again, philosophers of religion are not necessarily religious believers, and certainly most philosophers of art are not practising artists. Thus an important part of philosophical skill is to be able to describe what other people can probably do much more competently.

This raises another point about which there is often considerable misunderstanding. People whose expertise is in a particular subject are often highly suspicious of a philosopher who takes a professional interest in that subject yet has nothing like a comparable level of practical expertise in it. Thus, for example, dancers, and students and teachers of dance, sometimes express surprise that one should engage in a philosophical inquiry within their sphere of interest when one has never danced oneself, and is by no means a connoisseur of dance. It is this misunderstanding which partly explains why artists are sometimes suspicious of aestheticians. They seem to take the extreme view that a necessary condition of engaging in the philosophy of art is to be an artist. Yet I am certainly not suggesting that one can go to the opposite extreme and engage adequately in a philosophical consideration of a subject with little or no idea of what goes on in it, and of what its practitioners do and say about it.

Nevertheless, it is important to recognise that to philosophise adequately does not require an expert knowledge of the subject under consideration, since the philosophical perspective is of a different kind, and consists rather in describing the subject, and clarifying some of the problems which arise within it.

Thus philosophy can make a valuable contribution to the study of human movement by subjecting to logical scrutiny some of the statements made about the activities concerned, and by encouraging students to develop their ability for rigorously critical and independent thinking. This begins to reveal why misconceptions about the character and scope of philosophy can be so damaging. For instance, among the staff in physical education departments one sometimes encounters the belief that the philosopher is brought in to do the thinking for them, or to be critical of the way in which they do their work. Not surprisingly this may be resented as presumptuous, since they obviously have far greater knowledge of their own subjects. Yet it will seem presumptuous only if the proper concerns of the philosopher are not clearly understood. Unfortunately, some philosophers themselves contribute to this misconception, since they pursue their investigations in isolation from those in the field, and when they do appear they sometimes give the impression of rather condescendingly delivering the wisdom from on high. The attitude of such a philosopher can, perhaps, be captured by appropriating a quotation from Tennyson's 'The Palace of Art':

> I sit as God holding no form of creed,
> But contemplating all.

Much of the substance of the preceding discussion is a consequence of the fact that philosophy is continuous with general rationality, so that one could say of philosophy, as Popper (1971) has said of science, that it is merely common sense writ large. That is, philosophy is an extension of the reasoning which we all normally employ in everyday thinking and discussion, and to help us to formulate decisions. From this base of everyday reasoning the pyramid of philosophical thought is constructed, and it is important to remember that the upper levels of the pyramid are always dependent upon that base. The noted physicist and astronomer Hermann Bondi (1972) once remarked that a child has learned more physics by the time he is 3 years old than he will ever learn again. What he means by this is that a child of 3 has already made some of the most important advances in his grasp of physics, for example in learning about causation, simply by playing and experimenting with objects to see what happens to them in differing circumstances. Similarly, the child who is learning what makes sense and what does not; what counts as a reason, even in a simple case; and how to use language to express himself clearly, is already taking the most important steps towards a grasp of philosophy.

A SECOND-ORDER ACTIVITY

It may be helpful, if only initially, to think of philosophy as a second-order activity. This can be most clearly elucidated by means of examples. Let us first consider moral philosophy. The first-order activity is engaging in moral discourse or practices, and this will include recommending to other people what are their moral obligations, making moral decisions and acting upon them, formulating the ideals and moral principles by which one intends to live one's life, and criticising oneself and others for moral failure. By contrast, the moral philosopher operates on a higher logical level and is concerned not with substantive moral questions or injunctions, but with such questions as what people mean when they engage in moral discourse, what is the logical basis of moral judgements, and what sort of reasoning is employed in support of moral judgements. Similar considerations apply to the philosophy of religion. The first-order activity is that of engaging in religious practices, such as praying, going to church, and reading and discussing religious doctrines with a view to adopting them for oneself. The second-order activity of philosophy, on the other hand, is concerned with questions such as what people mean when they speak of God or life after death, and what sorts of reasons they adduce in favour of their religious beliefs. Again, the philosopher of science does not take part in scientific investigation or experiments in a laboratory but is concerned with the second-order analysis of the kinds of reasoning used in science, and, for example, precisely what it means, in this context, to say that A causes B. The philosopher of the arts is not a practising artist or critic, but considers problems such as 'What is art?' or 'How can a feeling be expressed in inanimate phenomena such as paint and canvas, or the sounds which constitute music?'. These examples allow us to understand more clearly why the philosopher does not require any special expertise in the substantive first-order activity about which he is philosophising, since he is trying to describe or analyse what is going on when people engage in the activity.

The same point applies to a consideration of human movement from a philosophical point of view, and this reveals a major source of the confusion to which I referred above. For one would not, *as* a philosopher, presume to tell those whose expertise is at the first-order level how, for instance, they should choreograph or perform dances, or what should be the attitude of those who engage in sport, or what are the most effective teaching methods in gymnastics. However, as we shall see in succeeding chapters, those who are involved at the first-order level often make statements which require philosophical clarification.

Emmett (1968) suggests that instead of speaking of philosophy it would be clearer to speak of the *activity* of learning to philosophise. This has the merit of emphasising that philosophy is an active endeavour rather than a body of knowledge which has to be acquired. Just as one cannot learn to play tennis solely by listening to lectures on techniques and tactics, so one cannot learn to philosophise simply by hearing or reading what even the great philosophers have to say. In both cases, of course, it may be necessary to have expert guidance, but in neither case can one succeed without active participation. It is necessary to emphasise this point since there is a prevalent misconception that philosophy is what I should prefer to call the history of ideas, i.e. knowing what the great philosophers thought. Instead, philosophy should be regarded as the development of rigorous, critical, independent thinking, and this requires *practice*. The benefits in our present sphere of interest will quickly become apparent, for in the literature on human movement there are misconceptions and inconsistencies which could fairly easily be recognised by someone who has had even a quite limited practice in philosophical thinking. Moreover, as might be expected since the discipline is continuous with general rationality, we are all inevitably concerned with philosophical questions very frequently. Thus it is advisable to be able to recognise when a question is philosophical, and to have acquired some of the requisite techniques of thinking to consider it adequately. Indeed, in my view every educated person should have some acquaintance with the discipline since, as we shall see, the techniques and insights of philosophical inquiry can illuminate any academic subject, and enhance general clarity of thought.

MEANING AND SUBSTANTIATION

There are, to put it roughly, two major kinds of question which are the concern of philosophy. These are to ask of any statement under consideration, (1) precisely what it means, and (2) whether and how it can be substantiated. These two kinds of question are closely related, as we shall see in a moment. Indeed, although it would be beyond the scope of this book to consider the issue in the requisite depth, I would contend that ultimately substantiation cannot be coherently separated from meaning. Nevertheless, for expository purposes the distinction is helpful. Let us first, then, look at the question of meaning.

We shall consider in succeeding chapters examples of confusions about the meanings of terms which invalidate scientific conclusions. It is also true, and common experience, that unnecessary disagreements sometimes arise because of such confusions. An example is provided by the philosopher William James who, on returning from a walk while on a camping holiday, found other campers engaged in a dispute concerning a man, a squirrel and a tree. On one side of the trunk of the tree clung a squirrel, but since the man was on the opposite side he was unable to see it. The others urged him to look at it so he walked round, but the squirrel also moved round the trunk in such a way that although the man circled the tree several times he was unable to catch sight of the elusive animal. The ensuing argument arose in response to the following question: The man went round the tree, and the squirrel was on the tree, but did the man go round the squirrel? William James was invited to adjudicate. He pointed out that the answer to the question depended upon precisely what was meant by asserting that the man went round the squirrel, or more specifically, what was meant by 'going round' in this context. If 'going round' meant that the man passed successively from positions first south of the animal, then west, then north, then east, then south again, then clearly he did go round the squirrel, since the squirrel was on the tree and the man successively passed through each of these positions relative to the tree. If, on the other hand, 'going round' meant that the man passed successively through positions first facing the front of the squirrel, then one side of it, then its back, then the other side of it, and then its front again, then clearly the man did not go round the squirrel, since he never occupied these positions relative to it. Once the distinction between the two senses of 'going round' becomes clear the dispute is dissolved rather than resolved, since it transpires that neither apparently opposing faction in the dispute was disagreeing with what the other meant by the term. Thus in fact there was no genuine disagreement between them.

It is interesting that some of the disputants, after this explanation, were frustrated by William James's failure to offer a definitive solution, and complained that he was merely quibbling with words. They insisted that they meant just plain English 'going round' and still wanted a clear answer to the question, rather than a typical philosophical evasion. Unfortunately, philosophers encounter this kind of unintelligent or uninformed criticism all too often, and frequently by people who ought to know better. It is important to avoid the misapprehension of regarding philosophising as *merely* a matter of playing with words and word meanings. A simple example was chosen in order to make the point clearly, but it should not be assumed that it reveals philosophy as concerned with verbal trivialities. Later chapters will reveal serious errors which can arise as a result of failure to be clear in the use of words. We shall return to this issue, but let us first consider the second major kind of question asked in philosophy, namely that which concerns substantiation.

There are two familiar methods of substantiation, which, for convenience, we can divide broadly into the empirical and the logical. Empirical substantiation is provided, as Emmett (1968) puts it, by 'going and seeing', i.e. by the gathering of information, or by investigation. It is in this way that one would answer questions such as: Are there any mushrooms growing in the field? How wide is the carpet? How many elm trees remain in the copse?

Scientific procedures are more sophisticated, more formal and systematised forms of the empirical. The sciences are concerned with answering more complex questions, or giving more precise answers, by rigorous investigation, by quantification, and by experimenting. For example, the rate of acceleration of falling objects is ascertained by scientific methods.

The second method, the logical, of which the philosophical is a species, is, roughly, substantiation by means of argument or reasoning concerning the meaning of the terms in question. A clear example of logical substantiation, although it is not philosophical, is the proof of a theorem such as the Pythagoras, in Euclidean geometry. It follows logically, by steps of deductive reasoning from the axioms and rules of inference, that the square on the hypotenuse of a right-angled triangle is equal in area to the sum of the squares on the other two sides. One does not carry out an empirical investigation into various right-angled triangles in order to substantiate the conclusion. Given the axioms and rules of inference it follows as a matter of logic.

An example which is rather nearer to philosophy concerns the substantiation of the assertion: 'A bachelor cannot have legitimate children.' This example reveals the close relationship of questions of substantiation and questions of meaning in philosophy, for to justify this assertion requires a consideration of the meaning of the terms used in it. This could be done as follows: a bachelor is an unmarried man; a legitimate child is the child of married parents; therefore a bachelor cannot have legitimate children. Again, it is unnecessary to carry out an empirical investigation, such as a sociological survey of bachelors, in order to substantiate the assertion. Although this is a simple example, it also illustrates the important point that philosophical or logical inquiry certainly involves discovery, in that as a consequence it is possible to learn and understand more about the world, but, unlike empirical investigation, this is not achieved by the collection of additional information. Philosophical inquiry provides understanding by considering the *nature* of the information which we already have, what it *amounts to*, or what it *means*.

It is probably already evident that it is often impossible to separate empirical from logical inquiry, for inevitably language is employed in scientific investigations. Thus the philosopher may be able to point out that, because of a confusion about the meanings or logical implications of the terms he is using, the scientist is not measuring what he thinks he is measuring, and therefore his conclusions, despite impeccably accurate observation and calculation, may be invalidated. There are various ways in which logical questions may have a significant bearing upon scientific investigations and thus it is advisable for those whose primary concern is with the latter to be increasingly aware of the contribution which can be made by philosophy.

It is often difficult to recognise the dependence of the empirical on the logical. For example, consider the question: 'Could a rose grow on the moon?' It may seem that this is a straightforward empirical question, to be resolved by the experiment of planting a rose on the moon and observing whether it grows. But further consideration reveals that the issue is not as simple as that, since it also raises questions of meaning or logic. Bambrough (1968) puts the point in this way:

> If we were to place what looked like a rose tree into the barren rock on the moon's surface, and it grew and flourished there, we should have strong reason to doubt its claim to be an ordinary rose tree. Anything that was *unquestionably* a rose tree would wither and die in the absence of atmosphere, moisture and soil. On the other hand, if we equip the moon with atmosphere, moisture and soil, so that ordinary roses would grow there, we shall be changing it so radically that in the end it will become doubtful whether it is still the moon on which the roses are now growing and blooming.

The point is that if it grew in the conditions of the moon's surface this would raise serious doubts about whether we could *call* it a rose, since what we normally call roses certainly could not grow in such conditions. On the other hand, if conditions on the moon were discovered to be such that ordinary roses would grow there this would inevitably raise serious questions about the concept of the moon, i.e. roughly, what we *mean* by the term 'moon'.

We need now to clarify the important notion of a concept, but first let us briefly see how some of the methods outlined so far can be applied more directly to human movement.

EXAMPLES

As an illustration, let us consider some very simple examples of ways in which a critical approach can help to encourage more careful thought about claims made for the value of movement education. I heard these claims made in a particular lecture, but they are typical of assertions which are often encountered.

(1) 'Movement should be an important part of every child's education since it is vital to life, so in making children more aware of movement we are making them more aware of life.' There are at least three ways in which this statement can be shown to be questionable:

(a) A parity of argument gives us: 'Eating is vital to life, so in making children more aware of eating we are making them more aware of life.' No one, presumably, as a consequence, would want to contend that eating education should be included in the curriculum. Other equally legitimate substitutions are, for example, 'drinking', 'oxygen', and 'blood', and there are many others. Thus it certainly cannot be assumed that simply because it is vital to life, an activity should be included in education.

(b) There is an illegitimate conflation of two senses of 'movement' here. This issue will be considered in Chapter 2, but, in brief, the kinds of movement which are vital to life, such as breathing, are not those which are the concern of the movement educationist, and the latter are not vital to life.

(c) Although it is true that to become aware of movement is to become aware of life, it is equally true that to become aware of anything at all is inevitably to become aware of life since life is, quite literally, everything that there is. So although the statement is necessarily true, it does nothing to show the value of movement in education.

(2) 'Movement experience is beneficial to children emotionally. This has been proved experimentally by the effects on emotionally maladjusted children.' Let us ignore the empirical part of this claim, i.e. concerning the experimental evidence, and ask whether, even if this is accepted, the conclusion is justified. And it can readily be seen that it is not justified. This is a common form of fallacious argument of which one should be aware, namely that of moving illegitimately from the particular to the general. In this case, it does not follow that what is beneficial for the emotionally maladjusted will necessarily be beneficial for all children.

CONCEPTS

This is an appropriate point at which to offer an initial elucidation of the notion of a concept, since it is a prerequisite for understanding the distinctive linguistic interests of the philosopher. Moreover, it is important that the use of the term 'concept' and its cognates should be clearly understood since they are widely employed in philosophy, and have a crucial bearing on many of the issues to be considered in later chapters. Thus the notion will be further clarified in Chapters 4 and 5. A misunderstanding of the term may also engender unnecessary disagreement when, as in Chapter 4, arguments are adduced to show it to be perfectly possible to be expert in the practical performance of a physical activity without having any grasp of the *concept* of that activity; and conversely to have no practical expertise yet a far better grasp of the relevant concept than the expert performer. It is significant in this respect that philosophical or logical analysis is sometimes referred to as conceptual analysis.

A natural and very common tendency is to regard a concept as a non-linguistic idea or thought, for instance in the mind of a speaker, which endows a word with meaning. But such a notion would reduce to incoherence, for if the meaning of a word were to depend upon its being 'backed' in this way by an idea or thought it would be impossible to know what it meant, since one could not delve into the speaker's mind in order to discover to which idea the word corresponded. Consequently there could be no way of knowing whether the idea which he associated with the word to endow it with meaning were the same as the idea which I associate with the word when he utters it. As this would apply equally to everyone else, no one could possibly know what anyone else meant by his use of words, hence there could be no communication, and the notion of language would be unintelligible. Indeed, the person who proposes this hypothesis is not entitled even to use the term 'word' because, to put the point paradoxically, apart from its recognised use as an interdependent part of an objective, public language, a word could not be a word, but would be merely an unintelligible sound or mark. Hence it transpires that the hypothesis is self-defeating, since the person who holds such a subjective theory of meaning, as dependent upon a correlation with purely private 'concepts' or 'ideas', cannot even state his case, as it would be impossible to understand him if his theory were correct. That is, in order to propose his thesis he has to *presuppose* what he is explicitly trying to deny, namely that verbal terms must have objective meanings as part of a public language. Therefore, to construe a concept as a meaning-entity in this way is incoherent.

The notion of a concept can be most clearly explained by comparison with meaning. To know the meaning of a word is to be able to use it correctly in a variety of contexts, but to have a grasp of the relevant *concept* is more a matter of knowing the logical consequences of the use of the word, and its relation to other concepts. The employment of the words 'more a matter' is significant in indicating that no sharp distinction can intelligibly be drawn between knowing the meaning of a term and having a grasp of the relevant concept. For example, a person could not be said to know the meaning of 'bachelor' if he did not know that a bachelor cannot be married. Yet he might be said to know the meaning of the word if he had not realised that a bachelor cannot have legitimate children. However, it is a logical consequence of the normal use of 'bachelor' that a bachelor cannot have legitimate children, which is to say that it is part of the *concept* of a bachelor. Hence the distinction is a matter of degree. To know the meaning of a word would certainly require a knowledge of *some* of its logical consequences, relations to other words, and implications, but to grasp the *concept* requires a more thoroughgoing awareness of these factors. The fact that a sharp distinction cannot be drawn between meaning and concept does not in the least vitiate its usefulness, since it would be absurd to suggest that in order to know the meaning of a word it is necessary to have a thorough grasp of its logical consequences. Nevertheless, the meaning of a word cannot, as we have seen above, be intelligibly considered in isolation, but only in relation to a whole set of logically interdependent terms which partly constitute a language. A *conceptual* inquiry is concerned to trace out some of those logical interdependencies in ways which are not normally required for knowledge of the meaning of a term, therefore it involves an examination of a whole cluster of related terms. Thus, for example, to examine the *concept* of freedom will inevitably include a consideration of related concepts such as causation, knowledge, responsibility and perhaps God. For it will be necessary to ask such questions as: If an action has been causally determined can it have been performed freely?; To what extent is lack of knowledge a limitation on one's freedom to act?; Is one responsible for an action only when it was freely performed?; If God be all-powerful, can people be free? It would not, of course, be necessary to have considered such questions carefully in order to be said to know the meaning of 'freedom' and its cognates.

Consequently it may be misleading to assume that there is a concept for every word. In many cases there is simply no point in employing the terminology since a word may have no significant logical consequences, and no relations to the uses of other words which raise questions of a philosophical nature. Incidentally, there are some other modern uses of the term which should not be confused with its use in philosophy. An example which I encountered recently was an advertisement for 'A new concept in breakfast cereals'.

PHILOSOPHY AND LANGUAGE

We are now in a position to begin to understand why it is a serious misconception to regard philosophy as mere quibbling with words. This common assumption is seriously misleading not simply because it misconstrues the nature of philosophy, but, far more damagingly, because it grossly oversimplifies and distorts the nature of language. Certainly the philosopher is centrally concerned with the logic of the language employed in different modes of inquiry, and in various forms of human activity. But his interest is not in the least like that of a lexicographer. On the contrary, the philosopher is concerned about the logic of language in these different areas of discourse in order to be clear about *what* it is which is being discussed or examined. In a very important sense that is far from being a concern solely with words, since the philosopher's interest in language cannot be distinguished from his interest in the world, with respect, for instance, to social and moral issues and to what counts as knowledge.

There is, of course, a great deal which could be said on this issue, since it is the most fundamental question of philosophy. I shall restrict myself to a brief account, partly because it raises the contentious issue of the subject matter of philosophy rather than the methodology, and therefore the conception of it which I shall outline is one with which some philosophers would want to disagree; and partly because the issue will become clearer as we consider some of the problems which arise in later chapters, and especially Chapter 8. (For a more detailed discussion of the topic see Winch, 1958, especially Chapter 1, and Hacking, 1975.)

A very important function of philosophy is, as we have seen, that of clarifying linguistic confusions, and pointing out inconsistencies and ambiguities. Some philosophers believe that this is the sole province of philosophy and, following Winch (1958), I shall refer to such a view as the 'underlabourer' conception. The title is derived from a passage in Locke, who held that genuine advances in knowledge are provided solely by empirical discovery, and for the philosopher: 'it is ambition enough to be employed as an under-labourer in clearing the ground a little and removing some of the rubbish that lies in the way to knowledge' (*Essay Concerning Human Understanding*). Although this function is important, it is, in my view, a mistake to regard it as the only contribution which can be made by philosophy, for there are questions which are raised specifically *within* philosophy, and which are not problems of clarification in the service of other disciplines. And that is to say that philosophy also has its own subject matter. The two major areas of such subject matter are metaphysics and epistemology. These areas are so interdependent that it is difficult to give separate characterisations of them. But, so far as this is possible, one could say that metaphysics, in this sense, concerns the ultimate grounds of knowledge and what counts as logic and reason. The fundamental question of epistemology, 'How could one know?' serves to test or reveal the underlying metaphysical assumptions. Thus, for instance, where the epistemological question reveals that it is not possible even in principle to justify an assertion, that is sufficient to show the assertion to be meaningless. As Winch puts it, 'the philosopher's interest in language lies not so much in the solution of particular linguistic confusions for their own sake, as in the solution of confusions about the nature of language in general'. A clear illustration was provided in the previous section, where a general theory of meaning in language was exposed by the epistemological question as depending upon untenable metaphysical assumptions. The theory asserts that the meaning of every word is given by a corresponding private 'idea' in the mind of the speaker. Yet the epistemological question of how it could be known that words are 'backed' in this way by private 'ideas' revealed the impossibility, even in principle, of justifying such an assertion. Thus the theory, and the metaphysical assumptions on which it depends, are shown to be incoherent. This issue will be further explored in Chapter 8.

The philosopher's central concern, in contrast to the linguistic interests of the lexicographer, is with the fundamental metaphysical question of the relationship of language, thought, and perception to reality, or, to put the point simply, that of man to nature. Thus the philosopher considers the question of the way in which language determines man's conception of what reality *is*. It is clear from the previous section that concepts are given with language, and in Chapter 8 it will be shown that there is a sense in which such conceptualisation at least partly *determines* reality, and cannot, as is commonly supposed, consist merely in a picture or reflection of reality. I raise the point briefly now to show that the consideration of such issues is certainly not an 'underlabourer' task for philosophy, but, on the contrary, they are considered in no other mode of inquiry. Winch (1958) puts the point in this way:

> We cannot say . . . that the problems of philosophy arise out of language *rather than* out of the world, because in discussing language philosophically we are in fact discussing *what counts as belonging to the world*. Our idea of what belongs to the realm of reality is given for us in the language that we use. The concepts we have settle for us the form of experience we have of the world . . . there is no way of getting outside the concepts in terms of which we think of the world . . . The world *is* for us what is presented through those concepts.

This also briefly indicates the importance of the issue to be raised in later chapters concerning the different but equally objective points of view from which an object or activity might be considered. Language, through its implicit conceptualisation, gives various objective ways of looking at the world, such as, for instance, the scientific, the moral, and the aesthetic. Yet these different frames of reference are still answerable to language. For it is only by reference to his ability to use the relevant linguistic terms that we can determine someone's ability to understand the point of view in question. Consequently, the view one takes of the fundamental metaphysical question of the relationship of language to reality will determine one's view of the other major areas of philosophical inquiry, such as philosophy of science, philosophy of religion, moral philosophy and aesthetics. Thus, as Winch says: 'The motive force for the philosophy of science comes from within philosophy rather than from within science. And its aim is not merely the negative one of removing obstacles from the path to the acquisition of further scientific knowledge, but the positive one of an increased philosophical understanding of what is involved in the concept of intelligibility.' A brief discussion of the way in which the metaphysical question of the concept of reality can determine the character of scientific facts will be included in Chapter 5.

I should introduce a note of caution about my use of the term 'metaphysics'. In the rest of this book I shall not use it in the sense explained here, but in the sense of that which is not in principle answerable to sense-perception. In this sense one would refer to the quasi-religious or poetic sense of philosophy outlined above as metaphysical. In order to provide a reminder of the way in which I use it, I shall refer to such a conception by the use of terms such as 'misty' or 'cloudy' metaphysics, in order to make clear that in my view it is not genuinely explanatory.

To return to the main point, there is, despite the fundamental issues discussed above, a persistent misapprehension that philosophy is merely quibbling with words. It is partly for this reason, and partly because some philosophers of the analytic and linguistic schools have, in my view, engaged in rather sterile discussions of fine but unimportant distinctions of meanings, and have thereby albeit unwittingly lent support to this misapprehension, that I prefer not to employ those terms to refer to my own work. However, this is not to deny the valuable contribution which has been made by many philosophers of these schools, and my own enormous debt to them.

SLOGANS

A damaging misapprehension, to which I have already briefly referred, which is sometimes encountered among those in the field of physical education or human movement is that of regarding the philosopher as a sort of academic witch-doctor whose role is to provide proof of the value of the practical activities concerned in the form of crisp, memorable slogans, or unassailable doctrines. Such an attitude derives, of course, from the mistily metaphysical conception of philosophy which we considered at the beginning. Those imbued with such a misconception tend to counter a slogan, or set of slogans, with another, and thus they perpetuate the misapprehension that to engage in philosophy is to acquire and be able to quote maxims thought out by the professional, or, worse still, by someone with practical expertise but little or no rigorous philosophical training. Much of the literature on the so-called philosophy of dance, sport and physical education can be shown, even on a cursory examination, to amount to no more than a string of pretentious slogans. This serves to perpetuate the common misconception about the nature of philosophy which I have tried to expose, since, as I hope is now clear, what in fact is required is to move out of the realm of sloganising altogether, and to begin on the constructive task of subjecting such slogans to critical examination.

One should be cautious, too, of those authors who refer to and quote from many academics of genuine repute. A long and distinguished reference list is certainly no guarantee of a soundly argued thesis. Moreover, some authors conduct their readers on a journey through 'idealism', 'realism', 'pragmatism' and any other 'ism' which may appear to confer academic respectability on their work. In discussion, too, the attempt is sometimes made to impress an audience with supposed erudition by introducing a bewildering range of 'isms'. It is ironic that readers and audiences are so easily impressed in this way since such a facile employment of the terms usually indicates an inadequate grasp of the complexity of the issues involved. One suspects that such a style is adopted in order to 'do a snow job' on the gullible, to borrow a picturesque American phrase. It has been aptly remarked that it is necessary to learn a third language in order even to attempt to understand what such people purport to be saying. Of course this is not to suggest that all literature which employs such terms is of dubious academic merit, but nevertheless one should be wary, and develop the confidence and ability to ask critical questions to establish whether anything of substance is being said. Experience increasingly confirms my conviction that there is no such thing as a clear idea which cannot be clearly expressed. Most technical terms can be avoided with the advantage of greater clarity for both reader and author, and even where, for economy of exposition, such terms are unavoidable, they should be clearly explained in non-technical language. This applies, of course, not only to philosophy. The literature in some other academic fields, such as sociology and branches of educational theory, is sometimes guilty of quite gratuitous obscurity, and again one often wonders about the value of the residue if the terminological excesses were expunged. One suspects that such a style is often adopted in order to avoid uncomfortable questions. This is where a genuinely philosophical approach can be so valuable, in uncovering disguised nonsense, to adapt Wittgenstein's remark again. It is surprising, in this respect, how often people are impressed because they cannot understand. This is not to deny, of course, that obscurity is sometimes unavoidable because of the complexity of the issues involved. Nevertheless, it should be remembered that there are two possible reasons for difficulty of comprehension:

(1) The unavoidable problem of formulating clearly a complex contribution of academic substance.
(2) Obscure presentation which may give a false impression of academic substance, but in fact says little or nothing.

It is my distinct impression that a good deal of the confused debate which takes place within the field of human movement stems from a failure to distinguish the latter from the former. As a consequence, reputations have been gained by making the obvious unintelligible, and the banal appear profound. To adapt Alexander Pope: 'In clouded majesty here dullness shone.'

PHILOSOPHICAL ANSWERS

What exacerbates the problem discussed above is the impossibility, in philosophy, of providing the concise, definitive answers which are the only kinds of answer which many people will accept. For example, no such answer could be given to the questions: 'What is aesthetics?' and 'What is mind?' since the concept of mind and the area of inquiry which comprises aesthetics are so complex. Hence any attempt to provide a concise answer will inevitably be misleading, which is why, as we shall see in Chapter 6, caution should be exercised about definitions. For although there is a persistent assumption that clarity of meaning can be achieved only by definition, the demand for a definition is often in effect a demand for distorting oversimplicity.

It is, of course, equally important to avoid the opposite danger, pointed out above, of indulging in unnecessary complexity. If a question is simple then of course a simple answer should be provided. But the questions which characteristically arise in philosophy are complex, hence the demand for a simple answer is in effect a demand for a false answer.

The point may be illustrated by a topographical analogy. There are small- and large-scale maps, giving either comprehensive grasp at the cost of oversimplification, or detail at the cost of a loss of comprehensive grasp. Philosophy is concerned with the careful consideration of problems, thus it is more akin to the large-scale map. People sometimes become exasperated by the careful reasoning and self-discipline required for a rigorous philosophical examination of a problem, and impatiently ask simply for the conclusion. This is rather like someone who wants to know what North America is like and, when provided with various maps showing respectively the topography, climate, geology, distribution of population, industry and natural resources, etc., he is dissatisfied because he wants one simple map which incorporates all this detail. It is as incoherent a request as the request for a philosophical conclusion without the argument, since, in an important sense, it is not the conclusion which is important in philosophy, at least in many cases, but the argument which leads to it. Or, to put the point another way, the notion of an answer to a philosophical problem may be misleading since it is the nature of the reasoning employed in the argument, rather than some concise conclusion, which *constitutes* the answer.

In the final chapter of *Without Answers* (1969), Rhees expresses the point in this way:

> This is why it would be absurd to look about for something to help you *over* the hard way so that you might enjoy the goal which is really important. 'Important' and 'hard' are inseparable here. (Not because in doing something hard you prove your own capacities, or anything of that sort.) . . . The philosophical difficulties have to be met and worked through. There is no sort of simplification, which will make them any less difficult . . . If you see the kind of difficulty that is raised in philosophy, you will see why there cannot be a simplified way of meeting it . . . Unless you feel like taking philosophy *seriously*, then leave it alone. And this means: take the *difficulties* seriously . . . Contrast: 'There are some rather tortuous difficulties here, but we need not go into these. We just want to get the general idea'. Whatever else that is, it is not philosophy.

'PHILOSOPHY' OF SPORT AND PHYSICAL EDUCATION

It may already be apparent that one of the principal reasons why I have felt it important to outline the character of the discipline is to draw attention to the dangers inherent in the gap which exists between genuine academic philosophy and much of the so-called 'philosophy' of physical education and sport. The latter often consists in little more than a statement of the author's beliefs about the value of the activities concerned, without critical examination, and it is difficult to see any justification for including that sort of enterprise in an academic course. Within an academic milieu it is surely illegitimate, as well as highly suspicious, that the 'philosophy of sport' and 'philosophy of physical education' should so often operate as autonomous areas of study, in isolation from the mainstream of philosophy, while apparently trading on the name 'philosophy' for academic respectability. This is as absurd and conducive to serious misconception as it would be if the physiology of exercise were to be studied in isolation from physiology, or the psychology of sport from psychology. As we have seen, philosophy is a matter of logical, rational justification, thus to exclude it opens the door to charlatanism. This isolation from philosophy no doubt explains why there is so much poor literature in the field, which continues to detract from the credentials of human movement as a genuinely rigorous area of academic study.

Philosophical examination may reveal that cherished beliefs have to be reconsidered, modified, or even abandoned, and this can be uncomfortable and disconcerting. Yet if such beliefs cannot be substantiated they *should* be modified or abandoned. A former colleague once complained that philosophy allows no place for conviction, but, as I hope is clear, there is certainly a place for conviction, but only when it can be justified. This has important implications not only for academic rigour, but also for sincerity, as we shall see. This complaint is related to the common misconception that modern philosophy is merely negative and destructive. Certainly rigorous critical examination is important, but to regard it as necessarily negative reveals not only a failure to understand the discipline of modern philosophy, but also, more seriously, a failure to understand the character of *any and every* academic discipline. Collingwood (1938) observes that it is often mistakenly believed that when a theory has been disproved it is necessary to begin again right back at the beginning, with the same initial question.

To a person who knows his business as a scientist, historian, philosopher, or any kind of enquirer, the refutation of a false theory constitutes a positive advance in his enquiry. It leaves him confronted not by the same old question, over again, but by a new question, more precise in its terms and therefore easier to answer. This new question is based on what he has learned from the theory he has refuted.

The point may be more fully elucidated by comparing the philosophical with the scientific method. The scientist proposes or considers a hypothesis which he subjects to searching empirical tests. That is, in effect he tries to *refute* it. In the same way a philosopher proposes or considers an argument or theory which he attempts to refute, but by logical, not empirical, testing. It is odd that the philosopher is thereby accused of being negative and destructive, yet one never hears of a similar complaint being levelled at modern scientists. This seems to confirm the suspicion of the persistent and widespread misapprehension about the character and contribution of philosophy to which I have drawn attention, namely that it should be concerned with offering doctrines and value-judgements.

Paradoxically, there are two prevalent yet incompatible extremes of misconception about philosophy: (1) that it is very remote and abstruse—the ultimate 'ivory-tower' subject, which promotes suspicions that it is 'airy-fairy' and of no practical relevance; and, by contrast, (2) that anyone can do it—there are bar-parlour philosophers but not bar-parlour physicists. One wonders how those with this latter attitude imagine undergraduates spend their time when reading for a degree in philosophy. It may explain why so many authors and speakers on practical aspects of physical education seem to feel no compunction about pronouncing on philosophical issues on the basis of no knowledge of the discipline. They would, quite rightly, be outraged if, solely on the basis of a philosophical training, one were to pronounce on, for instance, teaching dance or gymnastics in the primary school.

To repeat the point since it is so widely misunderstood, in its role as a second-order activity it is beyond the scope of philosophy to offer justification for beliefs about the value of physical activities. Questions of value cannot be settled by philosophical arguments alone, although certainly a philosophical examination may help to clarify some of the issues involved and it may explain how value-judgements can be supported by reasons. But it is not philosophy which decides whether particular reasons will or should lead to particular attributions of value.

IMPORTANCE OF INDEPENDENT, CRITICAL THINKING

Education, and especially higher education, should not, in my view, consist primarily in accumulating a stockpile of other people's thoughts and ideas, but rather in developing the ability for clear, critical, independent thought, and the demand, from oneself and others, for rational justification. As a result of the traditional conception of education, which might be stigmatised as the tyranny of the fact, it is still unfortunately true that too many students leave the college or university supermarket with carrier-bag minds filled with pre-packed ideas. This, in my opinion, is a travesty of what education should be. G. M. Trevelyan once said: 'Education . . . has produced a vast population able to read—but unable to distinguish what is worth reading.' The point is aptly made in a newspaper article criticising the preconception, revealed for instance in various radio and television contests, that education, or 'brain' power, consists in the ability to answer correctly numerous questions of unrelated fact:

> It is an assumption which has sold countless generations of parents countless sets of encyclopaedia and has made miserable the lives of all those students who, priding themselves on their logical, critical or creative faculties, have been floored by uncles saying things like, 'call yourself educated, and you don't even know which country's flag has a different design on each side?'.

This is certainly not to suggest, of course, that students should ignore what is written and said by those who have spent years working and researching in their subject of study. The point concerns the emphasis on the way in which students should be encouraged to approach what those with greater knowledge may have to offer. For, to return to the point mentioned above, the critical and independent thinking which is such an important characteristic of philosophy, as of other academic disciplines, is not only *not* negative and destructive but, on the contrary, is directly related to the constructive ability to be fully sincere, in thought and feeling, since there is an intimate relationship between rationality and the capacity for emotional depth. The point underlies this trenchant remark by Oscar Wilde:

> The intellectual and emotional life of ordinary people is a very contemptible affair. Just as they borrow their ideas from a sort of circulating library of thought . . . and send them back soiled at the end of each week, so they always try to get their emotions on credit, and refuse to pay the bill when it comes in.

This is a principal reason for my conviction that the most important contribution of higher education is, or should be, the encouragement of the ability to question perceptively, and think critically and objectively. The philosopher Kant drew attention to the close connection between rationality and morality. His point was that one cannot be fully sincere, about oneself or to others, unless one has developed the capacity and compulsion to ask *oneself* some searching questions, and to be able objectively to appraise the reasons adduced in support of the answers. Trow (1976) makes the perceptive point:

> There is a powerful morality implicit in the canons of verification, in our scholarly and scientific methods and procedures. This is perhaps most clear in our commitment to the search for negative evidence. The academic disciplines embody, in their methods of

work, procedures designed to force their practitioners to confront inconvenient facts ... The search for negative evidence and the decision to confront it and its implications for our current views are moral acts. Because these are virtues not merely of the scholar or scientist: a respect for evidence and for contrary opinion are qualities of mind that we need throughout society, as we resist the terrible certainties and brutal simplifications of the fanatic, the doctrinaire, the bigot, and the demagogue.

This sort of view is also a central theme in Bronowski's *The Ascent of Man* (1973).

Of course, it is undeniable that to consider the stockpiling of other people's views as higher education, makes life much more comfortable for the lecturers and professors since they do not have to cope with awkward questions, and can rest on authority. Moreover, such stockpiling, although tedious, is far less demanding for the students, since learning to think critically and objectively for oneself requires far greater effort. As Bertrand Russell once said: 'most people would sooner die than think. And in fact they do.'

REFERENCES: CHAPTER 1

Bambrough, J. R., *Reason, Truth and God* (London: Methuen, 1968).
Bondi, H., 'The achievement of Sir Karl Popper', *The Listener*, vol. 88, no. 2265 (24 August 1972).
Bronowski, J., *The Ascent of Man* (London: BBC Publications, 1973).
Collingwood, R., *The Principles of Art* (Oxford: Clarendon Press, 1938).
Emmett, E. R., *Learning to Philosophise* (Harmondsworth: Penguin, 1968).
Hacking, I., *Why Does Language Matter to Philosophy?* (Cambridge: Cambridge University Press, 1975).
Popper, K. R., 'Conversation with Karl Popper', in *Modern British Philosophy*, ed. B. Magee (London: Secker & Warburg, 1971).
Rhees, R., *Without Answers* (London: Routledge & Kegan Paul, 1969).
Trow, M., 'Developing students morally', *The Times Higher Education Supplement* (26 November 1976).
Winch, P., *The Idea of a Social Science and Its relation to Philosophy* (London: Routledge & Kegan Paul, 1958).
Wittgenstein, L., *Philosophical Investigations* (Oxford: Basil Blackwell, 1953).

Suggested Additional Reading

Emmett, E. R., *Learning to Philosophise* (Harmondsworth: Penguin, 1968).
Hospers, J., *Introduction to Philosophical Analysis* (London: Routledge & Kegan Paul, 1956).

Rhees, R., *Without Answers*, especially chs 14 and 17 (London: Routledge & Kegan Paul, 1969).
Wilson, J., *Thinking with Concepts* (Cambridge: Cambridge University Press, 1963).

Chapter 2

The Slipperiness of 'Movement'

INTRODUCTION

An immediate difficulty in considering the various claims made for the value of movement or movement education is to discover to what activities those who speak and write of it are referring. In the first chapter a sketch was offered of the nature and scope of philosophy, and it is appropriate that in the second we should apply some of the methods which were outlined to an examination of the concept of movement which is our primary concern in this book. In particular, I want to draw attention to a frequently unrecognised confusion in the use of the term 'movement', which is often revealed in an inadvertent slide from a very general sense of the term to an implicitly more restricted sense. Above all, I hope to encourage critical questioning of the claims so often made for the value of movement in education, and of what can properly be regarded as falling within the province of the study of human movement.

WIDE 'MOVEMENT'

A common form of argument starts by trying to show that movement is of an ineluctable, universal importance which extends even to inanimate objects. Thus Russell (1958) says: 'We live in a world of movement: the whole universe is in constant motion, all living things are in a state of gradual evolution and growth, there is ebb and flow in water and wind.' Similarly Gates (1968) writes, 'all around us in the world in which we live is movement—the coming and going, shifting and changing of all living things. It is in the forces of nature with their ceaseless fluctuations in time and space.' She writes later of the rising and setting of the sun, and of rivers flowing into the sea. However, although apparently assumed to be obvious, it is difficult to understand how the implied conclusion is supposed to follow from such facts as these. For it is far from clear how a premise about the movement of inanimate phenomena, such as the universe itself, and trees, rivers and seas, is supposed to lead to a conclusion about the importance of human movement in an education programme. It is also true that all around us in the world is air, but I have never heard this seriously proposed as a reason for the inclusion of air education in the curriculum.

Many writers implicitly or explicitly restrict their discussion to human beings, and, perhaps, other animate creatures, but still operate with a misleadingly wide notion of movement. For example, Gates (1968) writes 'Wherever there is breath and heartbeat, there is movement', and later she says that the initial premise from which her search for the character of movement was launched was that 'movement is being alive—everything that we do—all that happens to us'. Russell (1965) says of movement: 'It is a manifestation of life itself . . . Even in apparent stillness there is much movement in the body—the beat of the heart, the contraction and expansion of the lungs and the nerve impulses coursing to the brain.' Meerloo (1961) states: 'People, too, however quiet and immobile they may appear, are in constant rhythmic movement.' Hope Smith (1968) writes of 'man's equation of the term "movement" with life itself'. North (1971) writes: 'In the seemingly static as in the obviously mobile, the same kinds of laws of movement operate—at the macrocosmic level, as well as at the microcosmic and at the material as well as the non-material.' In a similar vein, according to Thornton (1971) Laban believed that no true state of immobility is possible. Laban (1966) also wrote that: 'the whole world is filled with unceasing movement. An unsophisticated mind has no difficulty in comprehending movement as life.'

There are several misconceptions which stem from statements such as these, of which I shall concentrate on just two, which are, in fact, aspects of the same confusion. The former is epitomised in the assertion which we considered in Chapter 1: 'Movement should be an important part of every child's education since it is vital to life, so in making children more aware of movement we are making them more aware of life.'

But from the fact that the movements required for breathing, heartbeats etc. are vital to life, it certainly does not follow that children in school will necessarily benefit from engaging in the quite different sorts of movement implicitly advocated by the 'movement' devotees. In short, two quite different kinds of movement are conflated here, and this invalidates the argument.

The latter misconception is inherent in the view that no true state of immobility is possible. Now whether this putative inevitability of movement is supposed to be the result of the activity of atomic particles, or of the movements upon which human life depends, such as breathing, the mistake is of the same genus, namely that of confusing one sort of movement with another, or, perhaps, of trying to use 'movement' in an incoherently general sense. Yet it is immediately apparent that something has gone badly wrong here, for, in the way the term is used by these authors, it is impossible for anyone ever to be still. Although matter may consist of particles in constant motion, this certainly does not imply that cars, trees, mountains and people can never be still. If you were to ignore a red traffic light while driving, it is unlikely that the magistrate would be much impressed with a defence which consisted of pleading that since all things are in constant motion it was impossible for you to stop. On the latter interpretation, when a teacher tells an unruly class to sit still, she would be effectively telling them all to commit suicide, since this would involve a cessation of breathing, heartbeats and nerve impulses. Moreover, ironically, this view of movement could well be used as an argument *against* the inclusion of 'movement' in education, for, as a consequence, it could be said that we are all moving all the time anyway, since we are all breathing and our hearts are beating. Thus there is no need for separate 'movement education' since we shall have quite enough of it simply by breathing etc. during, for instance, the mathematics and history lessons. It is interesting to notice this slide from a very wide sense to an implicitly more restricted one within the works of one writer. For example, Bruce (1965) says: 'We are engaged in moving during the whole of our lives', yet Bruce and Tooke (1966) write: 'It is essential that a teacher does his best to acquire some practical experience of movement, as it is only in this way that real understanding will come and that he will be able to guide others.' However, according to Bruce's former interpretation of 'movement' this injunction to the teacher is unnecessary, since, according to her own argument he, like all the rest of us, cannot prevent himself from moving all the time. Hence, presumably, simply being alive will inevitably provide him with plenty of practical experience of movement. If it were argued against me that what is meant is that the teacher should extend his movement experience beyond these obvious ones, then the same point is implicitly conceded. For not just any movement which is out of the ordinary would count as part of a movement-education programme—for example, an extraordinary nervous twitch in the big toe of my left foot.

The slide between the two meanings becomes apparent when we notice that it is the principal concern of such writers to convince us of the benefits of movement education, i.e. as *compared* with other aspects of education. So it is clear that they are operating with a more restricted sense of the term than they themselves realise in their initial appeal to the universality of movement, in some enormously general sense.

A similar mistake is sometimes made with respect to scientific discovery. To take a classic example, Eddington (1928) argues that modern atomic physics has shown us that we are all gravely mistaken about what we have for generations taken to be solid objects, such as tables and chairs. He explains that although a table, for instance, may appear to be solid, the physicist has proved that in fact such an object is not solid at all, but, on the contrary, it consists almost entirely of empty space with a lot of tiny particles whirling about—a sort of mêlée of microscopic dodgems. But again something has gone badly wrong here, for when in normal usage we attribute solidity to objects we are not making any claim for or against this notion of their atomic structure. Instead, we are implicitly contrasting them with non-solid items such as water and butter. Perhaps the point could be made forcibly to anyone inclined to Eddington's view if one were to say: 'Well, since you insist that physics has revealed the myth of the solidity of objects, presumably that applies to my boots, so you can have no objection to my kicking you hard on the shin.' The point is that 'solid' is being used in two different senses here, and the failure to recognise this engenders a bizarre conclusion. This is a good illustration of one of the tasks of philosophy which was explained in Chapter 1, namely that of attempting to clarify a confusion created by different meanings of a term. For one certainly does not wish to deny that there is a valid point underlying the statement that tables and chairs are not solid. As Bambrough (1972) puts it:

> Eddington misunderstood the difference that it makes and should make to our ideas of chairs and tables to be told about atoms and electrons, but he was not wrong to suggest that it does make a difference and that the difference is important.

The valid point might be more clearly expressed by saying that modern physics has revealed that, contrary to what is commonly supposed, a solid object does not consist of a continuous mass of substance, thus we should change our model, or conception, of what it is to be solid. There are two senses:

solid 1 = resistant to touch and pressure, for example, tables and chairs, as opposed to water and butter.
solid 2 = roughly, continuously filled with matter.

Eddington confused these two senses, and thus he expressed what should have been a point about sense 2 as though he were denying solidity in sense 1. This led him to claim that physical theory had shown that the term 'solid', in sense 1, just could not intelligibly be said to apply to anything. In short, he was denying that there were any solid objects. In fact, to repeat the point, he should have been denying a certain picture of the physical *constitution* of solid objects.

To say, as Laban does, that no true state of immobility is possible is to be similarly confused, since there is an elision of two senses of 'movement' and its cognates, and this leads him to make illegitimate assumptions about the importance of human movement in his *particular* sense of that term. That is, Laban is implicitly or explicitly importing a conclusion which is justifiable in the context of discussion of the physical composition of matter, namely the conclusion that all matter consists of the incessant movements of particles, and illicitly employing that conclusion to persuade us of the importance of the quite different sorts of *human* movements with which he is concerned. In the former sense it may be correct to aver that no true state of immobility is possible, since that means that *all* matter consists of ceaselessly moving particles. But that gives no grounds at all for concluding that, in the latter sense, it is impossible for people ever to be immobile, or that, for instance, movement education is thereby rendered more important. If one were to adopt Laban's interpretation, to say of an energetic pupil, 'That boy never stops moving' would be as uninformative a truism as to say, 'That boy is a young male human being', since the boy is composed of matter, and all matter is, of necessity, incessantly moving.

Incidentally, Laban (1947) appears to be similarly confused over the concept of space, since he says: 'empty space does not exist. On the contrary, space is a superabundance of simultaneous movements.' On this view the gymnastics teacher who asks his pupils to fill the empty spaces is asking the impossible, but he would probably be annoyed if his pupils refused to do what they were asked on that account.

ILLEGITIMATE 'DANCE'

A more obvious case of slipperiness sometimes occurs with the term 'dance'. For example, in support of her argument that dance is the primary art, Russell (1969) writes of children 'dancing with joy and rage', and adds 'one recalls such pictures as that of Bobby Moore, leaping and dancing, World Cup in hand'. Similarly Meerloo (1961) states: 'Even in conversation people either "dance" toward or away from each other.' To her credit, Meerloo's inverted commas at least appear to show some lurking sense of uneasiness at using 'dance' in this way. For, of course, it is quite illegitimate to use such a metaphorical sense of 'dance' in support of an argument for the importance of dance in the more normal sense. That would be like advocating, as part of the education of the emotions, the inclusion in the curriculum of lessons on the use of gunpowder, on the grounds that people 'naturally' explode with anger, and of lessons on refrigeration techniques since people tend to become frozen with fear.

MORE RESTRICTED 'MOVEMENT'

Let us consider a slightly narrower, but still much too wide notion of 'movement', as exemplified by L. Schiller (preface to D. Jordan, 1966): 'Movement is not a new subject; moving, like talking, is a continuing exploration of what every boy and girl does from his earliest years.' In the same vein Bruce (1965) writes: 'A young baby lies in his cot absorbed in the discovery of his fingers and of his feet. A young child becomes increasingly aware of his body, the shape of that which he can see, and how parts will move. It is this early exploring which is to be developed in the rediscovery of parts of the body through movement education.' North (1971) tells us that movement education is not physical education, or dancing, or drama, and gives as her positive view: 'Movement is something which everyone knows a great deal about either consciously or simply by being in a state of motion, vibration or activity of some kind, all the time.' But it is hard to understand why, on this sort of account, the drill of the 'bad old days' can be excluded. After all, one has to move to perform drill— arm-stretching, knees-bending etc.—and in this way one can, often all too painfully, 'rediscover' parts of the body. Yet the very thought of including drill in education would appal most 'movement' enthusiasts. Similarly, in this sense, there is surely plenty to be discovered in formal gymnastics when performing such activities as handstands and backward rolls, yet the more extreme disciples of 'movement', often seem to regard such words as 'handstand' as almost obscene.

Another of the unnoticed shifts from a narrow to a wider sense of 'movement' often occurs in discussion of communication and expression. Thus, for example, Thornton (1971), in his account of Laban, says: '. . . some maintain that true expression begins where language ends and a profound emotional experience is often beyond words. Without movement there would be no outlet for any of the experiences which man undergoes.' Now the former sentence is implicitly contrasting the supposed richness of movement with the supposed poverty of language, as a means of expression, i.e. 'movement' is to be understood in a restricted sense. The latter sentence, however, implies that language, and indeed every other form of expression, is dependent upon movement of some sort, i.e. 'movement' is to be understood in a much wider sense which would *include* and therefore could not be compared with language.

There is another commonly encountered misconception implicit in the former sentence, which is that movement is generally superior to language as a means of expression and communication. This raises complex issues which we shall consider in Chapter 9, but it is immediately apparent that such an assumption is at least highly questionable since without language there could be, to name but a few examples, none of the intricate economic, industrial and political systems of modern society. Creatures without language can move, but it is significant that they are incapable of engaging in such systems, for which linguistic ability is necessary.

MOTION AND MOVEMENT

Thornton (1971) says that according to Laban there is a distinction between motion and movement, but on examination it proves difficult to understand this supposed distinction. Thornton writes: 'Laban believed that man, through his movement, is linked with the movements of the planets and matter and is part of the natural order of the universe.' Yet later he says that Laban believed that the movements of the natural world 'were not motion but movement since their path through space was dictated by natural law'. There is clearly something wrong here, for if man is part of the natural order, he is unable, on this account, to make any *motions*, they will all be *movements*, since everything he does will be 'dictated by the natural law'. More damagingly, presumably, since, according to Laban, everything else, for example planets and matter, is part of the natural order, there can be no 'motion'. In short, this seems to be a vacuous distinction, since Laban himself has already ruled out the possibility of 'motion'.

Another conception of movement, as opposed to motion, is that the former 'is not the mere motion of limbs and body in some haphazard way divorced from inner participation; it is the visible manifestation of man's true intellectual, emotional and spiritual state' (Thornton, 1971). We shall consider in later chapters the profound misconception concerning the body/mind relationship which is usually encapsulated in this sort of statement, but to put the point briefly, if the mental and the physical were to be separated in this way, there would be an insuperable problem about getting them together again, i.e. of ever knowing that a particular physical movement is 'backed' by the supposed 'intellectual, emotional and spiritual state'. For although there is obviously no problem about seeing the limbs and body, it does not make sense to suppose that one could, as it were, reach into the mind of the person concerned in order to find out whether the motion or movement is divorced from inner participation, or whether it is manifesting a mental state. Hence one could never distinguish between motion and movement. However, it might be that, although confused by an inadequate body/mind theory, Laban is here groping after a distinction between intentional actions and those which are non-intentional. This would certainly make some sense, although even if we restrict 'movement' to intentional actions, we shall still have far too wide a category for the sorts of movement which could reasonably be regarded as coming within the province of movement education. For example, to wink at an attractive girl is certainly an intentional action, but it is unlikely that such an action would be included in a movement-education programme.

MORE 'MOVEMENT' PROBLEMS

In addition to the foregoing, there are the following four considerations. First, it is obvious that a good deal of movement is harmful, so to use 'movement' in a wide sense might prove to be an embarrassment to movement devotees. There are, of course, cases of broken limbs and pulled muscles, death by over-exertion, and the movements involved in expressing anger, committing murder etc. Furthermore, those who make extravagant claims about the pre-eminent value of movement in developing man's cultural and intellectual life, should notice an interesting counter-example provided by Bronowski (1973), who, writing of the Bakhtiari, a Persian nomadic tribe, says:

> The Bakhtiari life is too narrow to have time for a skill or specialisation. There is no room for innovation, because there is not time, *on the move*, between evening and morning, coming and going all their lives, to develop a new device or a new thought—or even a new tune. The only habits that survive are the old habits. The only ambition of the son is to be like the father. (my italics)

So, for this tribe, as, no doubt for many others, movement is actually a *handicap* to development.

Secondly, it is no good saying that the only way we shall know what 'movement' means is to feel it, although this is a common ploy among the faithful. For we cannot do this until we know what we are supposed to feel. We shall consider this issue more fully in Chapter 6, but, to put the point briefly, in order to have any conception of a particular feeling, it must be possible to recognise its typical manifestation in behaviour.

Thirdly, how many of us have found that our ability to achieve a more profound understanding of ourselves and of many aspects of our lives has been achieved *not* by movement but, on the contrary, by learning the difficult art of being still? For the religious believer this is aptly expressed as, 'Be still and know that I am God', and learning to be still is an important part of Yoga. The significance of the point is recognised in the motto adopted by one British university: 'Be still and know.'

Fourthly, even if we should ignore all these problems and accept, even implicitly, a more restricted sense of 'movement', there would be difficulties. One of the greatest of these is the question of what is supposed to be the value of learning, or learning about Laban's and his followers' movement principles. According to Russell (1965), Laban 'helped us to appreciate that movement is fundamental in all life and that in man's efforts, whether functional or expressive, whether in large movements of the whole body or small unconscious movements of parts, there can be found common factors and fundamental principles'. Similarly, Bruce (1965), with reference to Laban's work, says: 'There exists a need for the training of fundamental concepts of movement as a basis for the athletic and gymnastic skills as for the arts of dance and dance drama.' Now this seems to mean that if we learn these general, or universal, movement principles, then it will be easier for us to develop specific movement abilities, for example in dance, squash or rowing. Yet this is flatly denied in Thornton (1971), who writes: 'Laban never suggested that a thorough physical training in the art of movement would automatically mean that specific skills would be learned more readily.' This is puzzling. One can at least understand the claim that learning the fundamental general principles will help one to acquire specific movement skills more easily, and it could be tested by rigorous and wide-ranging empirical examination. But if this is not what is meant, then just what *is* supposed to be the value of learning these 'common factors and fundamental principles'? If the contention should be that they are to be learned purely for greater theoretical understanding, then this should be clearly stated, and distinguished from the claim concerning the acquisition of particular practical skills of movement.

'BASIC MOVEMENT'

Another type of argument which is frequently employed depends on such notoriously slippery terms as 'basic', 'fundamental', and 'primary'. For example, Russell (1965) talks of movement as one of the first and a primary means of expression, and a basis of other forms of expression. From this sort of consideration she and many others take it that dance is the basic, fundamental, primary art form. If this were to mean simply that dance was, historically, the first of the art forms, then it would seem to be very difficult to establish the claim, since there would appear to be equally good grounds for claiming that drawing, carving or painting came first. But, more importantly, what is supposed to follow from this? One often encounters arguments, and advertisements, which vaguely imply that an activity, or a product, is somehow more important than or preferable to others simply because it came first. For example, a well-known toffee manufacturer advertises its product as 'the original and best'. Yet even if dance or movement did come first, that gives no grounds for claiming that it is now the most important art form, or even that it is worth pursuing at all. On a parallel argument we should, perhaps, abandon ocean liners and jet aircraft for our transport to overseas countries and revert to coracles, since they were the 'basic', 'fundamental', 'primary' way of travelling across water.

IMPORTANCE OF CLEAR 'MOVEMENT'

I am suggesting, then, that we should reject talk of 'movement' in some vaguely and possibly vacuously wide general sense. We need to know, at least roughly, what is the province of human movement, and of movement education. I am not saying, of course, that we need a sharp definition, since it is probable that no such definition could be found which would do justice to the variety and indefinite possibility of extension in a sphere of activity such as this. Moreover, I am certainly not suggesting that it should be possible to explain movement comprehensively in words, since, for instance, what is expressed in the medium of physical movement which is peculiarly the province of dance could not, as a matter of logic, be expressed in the different medium of words.

My point is that although it may not be possible to produce a *definition* of the meaning of the term 'movement' which is of interest to us, that does not prevent our having a fairly clear idea of what are the concerns of a department of human movement or human kinetics. After all, it is impossible to produce a verbal definition of the names of the primary colours, yet that does not prevent our knowing what 'red' means, and being able to apply it correctly. Just as we could point out various red objects to someone who wanted to know what 'red' meant, so we could show or explain to someone who did not know, the kinds of movement in which a department of human movement is interested. For example, we could explain to him that we are interested in the movements which are characteristically employed in various sporting activities, dance and physical education. Yet many of the writers whom I have quoted, and many more people in the field of 'movement', explicitly reject this, or, apparently, any other limitation, in which case they owe us an explanation of what sort of activities are to be included in the movement-education programme. For example, a very wide view would fail to exclude nervous twitches, reflex actions and the movement of the bowels.

No doubt, to the converted, this chapter may seem negative or even rebarbative, but it is certainly not my intention to be so. My overriding concern is to try to point out that unless we set some boundaries, even if they cannot be sharply delineated, to the meanings of 'movement' and 'movement education', and unless we can indicate how the claims made for the value of movement can be substantiated, either by scientific examination or by reasoned argument, then we are quite literally making no sense. It might be argued against me that there is more to life than mere cold scientific facts or reasoning. But it is interesting to notice that people who argue in this way put themselves in a paradoxically self-defeating position, since they themselves adduce reasons why reasoning is of limited application. A good deal of misunderstanding here arises from a distortedly narrow view of what constitutes genuine reasoning. The notion is still very prevalent that genuine reasoning must be either inductive (as, characteristically, in science) or deductive (as in mathematics). But there is far more scope for reasoning than that. For example, one can give reasons for an emotional reaction, for a moral judgement, for one's view of life, and for an aesthetic judgement, to name but a few instances, for none of which inductive or deductive reasoning is characteristically or at least exclusively employed. Nevertheless, one common and necessary feature is that such reasoning in these spheres or in any other must be answerable, at least in principle, to what could be perceived.

Moreover, I certainly do not wish to be understood as denying that movement education, in a restricted and therefore manageable sense (perhaps at least centrally located in the activities which are normally the province of enlightened physical education), is of value. On the contrary, the case for movement education can only be harmed by extravagant and mistily metaphysical claims. According to Thornton (1971), Laban averred that movement was 'more than a way of educating man. He believed that it was *the* way of educating through the arts.' There may be a case for arguing that education has tended, and perhaps still tends, to exaggerate the importance of the traditional academic subjects. However, even if that were true, the remedy is not, in turn, to exaggerate the importance of movement and the arts. To rectify imbalance one does not overweight the lighter side of the scales. There are good reasons why the development of linguistic skills has been, and should continue to be, the most important single aspect of every child's education, yet that is certainly not to say that language, or any other aspect, is *the* way of educating. There are many valuable areas of experience which should be included in education, among which are movement, physical education, dance. Perhaps some fervent, uncritical dedication was needed initially to set the 'movement' movement moving, but it should surely now be subjected to a less eulogistic, more realistic appraisal. Talking to followers of Laban often reminds one of talking to doctrinaire Marxists, Freudians and extreme fundamentalist religious believers. It seems to be taken as axiomatic that the Great Man could say no wrong—any errors or self-contradictions are hastily attributed to his followers' faulty interpretations, or to mistakes in translation. His acolytes would rather doubt their ability to understand The Master than question the validity of what he said. In my view this does both 'movement' and Laban a disservice, for although I have no reason to doubt that much of what he said is of considerable value, I equally have no doubt that some of what he said is, to say the least, highly questionable on philosophical, if not on 'movement' grounds. (It is encouraging that some critical works have appeared, for example Redfern, 1973.)

A significant additional point, which tends to be overlooked by the fervent, is that anyway we should be clear that personal issues are of little consequence. It is not important, except for a biographer, whether Laban did actually say or mean this or that. What is of the utmost importance to physical educationists is the validity of the ideas upon which the 'movement' programme is based.

MOVING TO A CONCLUSION

I have tried to show that it is only by using a sense so wide that it includes any and every conceivable sort of movement that any plausibility may be given to the huge claims sometimes made for 'movement' and 'movement education'—for example that every form of expression, indeed life itself, depends upon movement. But then, having won assent to what he says about 'movement' in this sense, the devotee slides inadvertently and unnoticed into a sense of 'movement' which is much narrower, as becomes evident when we recognise, for instance, that he now starts to compare movement favourably with other forms of expression. Or, to put the same point another way, the wide sense allows the claims, but eliminates all the distinctions by making all forms of expression into movement, yet the 'movement' apologist needs the distinctions in order to show what he takes to be the advantages of movement *vis-à-vis* other forms of expression. So he implicitly uses a narrower sense of 'movement', but illegitimately continues to import the claims which are allowable only for the wide sense. He cannot have it both ways. Either *every* form of expression is movement, in which case you may carry the large claims but they are empty since there is no other form with which to compare them, or movement is *one form* of expression among others, in which case the large claims no longer apply, so you have to make a new case for the value of movement. We should not be lulled into bland acceptance of the claims made for the former sense when they are sneaked in to support the latter. There is far more likelihood of producing a valid and convincing argument for the value of movement when we recognise how slippery 'movement' can be.

REFERENCES: CHAPTER 2

Bambrough, J. R., 'Appearance, identity and ontology', unpublished paper delivered at a general seminar of the Faculty of Philosophy, Cambridge University, 1972.

Bronowski, J., *The Ascent of Man* (London: BBC Publications, 1973).

Bruce, V. R., *Dance and Dance Drama in Education* (Oxford: Pergamon Press, 1965).

Bruce, U. R., and Tooke, J. D., *Lord of the Dance: An Approach to Religious Education* (Oxford: Pergamon Press, 1966).

Eddington, A., *The Nature of the Physical World* (London: Dent, 1928).

Gates, A., *A New Look at Movement—A Dancer's View* (Minneapolis: Burgess Publishing Company, 1968).

Jordan, D., *Childhood and Movement* (Oxford: Basil Blackwell, 1966).

Laban, R., *Choreutics* (London: Macdonald & Evans, 1966).

Laban, R., and Lawrence, F. C., *Effort* (London: Macdonald & Evans, 1947).

Meerloo, J. A. M., *Dance Craze and Sacred Dance* (London: Peter Owen, 1961).

North, M., *An Introduction to Movement Study and Teaching* (London: Macdonald & Evans, 1971).

Redfern, B., *Concepts in Modern Educational Dance* (London: Lepus Books, Henry Kimpton Publishers, 1973).

Russell, J., *Modern Dance in Education* (London: Macdonald & Evans, 1958).

Russell, J., *Creative Dance in the Primary School* (London: Macdonald & Evans, 1965).

Russell, J., *Creative Dance in the Secondary School* (London: Macdonald & Evans, 1969).

Smith, H. M., 'The nature of human movement', in *Introduction to Human Movement*, ed. Hope Smith (Reading, Mass.: Addison-Wesley Publishing Company, 1968).

Thornton, S., *A Movement Perspective of Laban* (London: Macdonald & Evans, 1971).

Chapter 3

Rhythm in Movement

INTRODUCTION

Those engaged practically in physical education, sport and dance, either as teachers or as participants, often maintain that the development of rhythm is an important factor in the accomplished performance of a wide range of physical activities. Certainly it is difficult to imagine how dance could be taught without recourse to the notion of rhythm, but it is also commonly employed in gymnastics, track and field events, and a great variety of other sporting activities. One speaks, for instance, of the rhythm of a sequence in gymnastics, of a swimmer's rhythm, of the rhythm of a service action in tennis, of the rhythm of a golf swing, of the rhythm of a jumper's run-up, and there are innumerable such examples.

Yet there reigns such confusion in the use of the term 'rhythm' that all too frequently it is by no means clear what quality or attribute is supposed to be predicated by it. The concept will be examined here in relation to the ways in which it is frequently employed by prominent writers on human movement. However, it should be emphasised that this lack of clarity in the use of 'rhythm' and its cognates is by no means limited to discussion of movement, physical education, sport and dance, since one finds a similar vagueness in its application to music, painting, and other arts. Nevertheless, in this chapter we shall concentrate specifically upon the concept of rhythm in its application to human movement in order to reveal the nature of the problem, which is commonly unrecognised by those who use the term; to propose at least an inchoate guideline which might facilitate a more consistent and coherent usage; but, above all, in the hope of stimulating further attempts to clarify a term which can be very useful, but which often seems to be used uncritically and with confusing consequences.

RHYTHM IN ALL MOVEMENT

The problem to which I advert is implicit in the statement, which often seems to be taken as an article of faith, that there is rhythm in all movement. I shall take this statement as my stalking horse. For example, H'Doubler (1946) writes that 'any movement, no matter how poorly co-ordinated or executed, has rhythm, but a rhythm that is different from that of the well co-ordinated performance'; Mettler (1942) remarks, 'All movement has rhythm, although the rhythm of certain movements may be more pronounced than that of others'; Jordan (1966) says that all human life is rhythmic by nature; Russell (1969) speaks of 'man's rhythmical nature'; and Bruce (1970) quotes Myers as saying, 'Movement and rhythm are insolubly linked together'. Now obviously such statements are not making any meaningful claim unless we know how the term is to be understood. So what does the word 'rhythm' mean? The *Concise Oxford Dictionary* gives the following four possible explanations:

(1) Metrical movement determined by various relations of long and short or accented and unaccented syllables, measured flow of words and phrases in verse or prose.
(2) That feature of musical composition concerned with periodical accent and the duration of notes.
(3) (Art) harmonious correlation of parts.
(4) (Physics, Physiol., and gen.) movement with regular succession of strong and weak elements.

It may well be that these accounts, either separately or together, do not add up to a strict definition in the sense in which a square may be precisely defined as an equilateral rectangle. There are, as we shall see in Chapter 6, very many terms of whose meanings we are well-enough aware but which are not susceptible of such stringent definitions. Nevertheless, with the possible exception of the third, there is at least one common characteristic which emerges from these accounts and which would seem to conform to what most of us would regard as a central feature of the correct use of the word 'rhythm'. The common characteristic is that of a recurring pattern of some sort.

However, if this should be a central feature of the correct use of 'rhythm' and its cognates, then it is by no means clear how it can justifiably be claimed that all movement is rhythmic. That is, it would appear that it cannot consistently be maintained both that rhythm requires a recurring pattern, and that there is rhythm in all movement. No doubt when a person walks or runs, to take simple examples, a recurring pattern, and therefore a rhythmic structure, can be discerned in his movements, and there are many such cases where a series of movements can be seen to fall into characteristic recurring patterns. Yet some movements or sets of movements are performed once only, in which case it is difficult to understand how they can be claimed to be rhythmic since there is no recurring pattern. For example, if I were to leap up from my writing and perform a back somersault over my desk, I should almost certainly be unable to perform that or, at least until after convalescence, any other movement again. Perhaps the point can be made even more obviously in the case of my performing a swallow dive, at low tide when the rocks are revealed, from a high cliff.

Now, if it should be objected that rhythm can be seen to occur within these movements when they are analysed into their constituent parts, then we can change the example. If I quite suddenly shoot my arm out at an unusual angle, just once, on what grounds could this movement justifiably be regarded as rhythmic? Some people who have heard my argument insist that there is rhythm even in such a very short, non-recurrent movement, but that it is impossible to detect it. Against this I would say, first, that we still have not been told what it is we are supposed to understand by 'rhythm', and therefore we still do not know what we are supposed to detect, and secondly, that if it cannot, even in principle, be detected how on earth could it be known to be present?

More commonly, some writers appear broadly and usually implicitly to accept this requirement of a recurrent pattern, but for their support for the claim that there is rhythm in all movement they depend upon scientific discoveries or cosmological theories about the nature of matter. For example, North (1971) writes: 'We all know intellectually that all created things are in constant motion—not just moving about, but in ordered, patterned, rhythmical motion. Our whole world depends upon this order of moving particles . . .' Similarly Meerloo (1962) writes: 'Tiny particles inside the atom dance their various orbits in an ultra-microscopic cosmos while in the greater universe stars and galaxies move along their immense pathways in steady continuity. Molecules are in continual agitation and tremor. People, too, however quiet and immobile they may appear, are in constant rhythmic movement.' This sort of argument is commonly encountered not only with respect to rhythm but also, as we saw in Chapter 2, with respect to movement generally. The illicit slide from the cosmic to the more restricted sense of 'rhythm' is precisely similar to the slide we considered with respect to 'movement'. That is, even if it be true that all matter consists in rhythmic movement, this cannot be cited to justify the statement that all human movement is rhythmic, since such a conclusion relies upon an illegitimate elision of two senses of the term 'rhythmic'.

A DIFFERENT SENSE OF 'RHYTHM'?

Another common line of argument would concede that, in the normal sense of the term, rhythm does not occur in all movement, but would insist that the rhythm in movement is of a different kind, which is not necessarily recurrent. The difficulty is to discover any clear and reasonably unified account of what this kind of rhythm might be. A distinction is sometimes drawn between metric and non-metric rhythm, but this involves problems of its own, since it is by no means clear what is meant by 'non-metric rhythm'. The distinction may be one of complexity—metric rhythms being relatively simple and sharply accented as in a waltz, and non-metric rhythms being of such a degree of complexity that it is difficult, especially for the layman, to discern them. For example, Jordan (1966) writes: 'It must not be supposed that rhythm only emerges in response to an audible beat or sound, for in most movement it is an inaudible factor.' If this is what is meant by the distinction, then it is not incompatible with the view that rhythm requires a recurring pattern, since there are some rhythms, for example in Indian classical music, which are very complicated indeed, although they involve recurring patterns. Moreover, I certainly would not wish to suggest that rhythm must be marked in some audible way. A high degree of complexity, then, is quite compatible with our account of the normal sense of 'rhythm'.

However, some writers conceive the distinction between metric and non-metric rhythm not in terms of a greater degree of complexity, but of a difference in kind. For example, Preston (1963) writes: 'There are two kinds of rhythm, metric and non-metric. The latter is also referred to as free rhythm and breath rhythm. Basically, it can be said that the rhythm of the legs in steps is usually metric, while the rhythm of gesture is usually non-metric.' It would appear that to use 'non-metric' or 'free' in this way effectively negates that characteristic of a recurring pattern which, I suggested above, is central to the normal meaning of 'rhythm'. For there are gestures, even in dance, which do not recur and are not part of a recurrent pattern. So that instead of saying that such gestures involve free or non-metric rhythm, it would seem to be less confusing to speak of them as *non*-rhythmic movements.

Certainly it is often the case that a word which has a central meaning may develop extended, peripheral or metaphorical meanings. For example, 'mouth', normally used to refer to an external orifice in the head, may be used of a river, and similarly one can speak of a bachelor girl, of brake shoes, and of hammering out an agreement. I shall consider more fully below the notion of an extended sense, but the point I wish to make now is that although no sharp limits can be set to the possibilities of such extensions of meaning, that is certainly *not* to say that there are *no* limits. There is surely a case for arguing that the limits have been exceeded where the word is used in a way which denies the principal distinction marked by the central meaning. Thus it seems at least odd, on the face of it, to use the terms 'non-metric rhythm' and 'free rhythm' to refer to movement which, in the normal sense, manifests *no* rhythm.

Moreover, it remains unclear what precisely is the significance of claiming that all movement is rhythmic. In their defence of this claim some people seem to slide, albeit inadvertently, into a position which removes *all* substance from the word 'rhythmic'. Perhaps I can make the point more clearly by means of an example. Let us suppose that it is claimed that all swans are white, and subsequently a creature is produced which is in every respect indistinguishable from a swan except that it is black. Those who proposed the original claim may react in any of the following ways:

(1) They may simply accept this as a counter-example which refutes their original contention by showing that there is at least one swan which is not white.
(2) They may continue to insist that all swans are white, and that therefore this cannot be a swan.
(3) They may continue to maintain their claim by averring that, despite appearances, this swan *is* white, although not in the normal sense of the term 'white'.

Analogously, if we produce a movement in which no recurring pattern can be discerned there are three possible reactions:

(1) It could, and surely would normally, be taken as a counter-example which refutes the original contention by showing that some movement is not rhythmic.
(2) The second analogue, of denying that this can be a movement on the grounds that it is not rhythmic, has not, as far as I am aware, been seriously proposed.
(3) The third analogue *does* appear to be adopted quite often, although no doubt inadvertently, by those who seem to regard the universal statement as an article of faith. It is said, in effect anyway, that since this is movement, it *must* be rhythmic, even if not in the normal sense of that term. The problem is that usually we are not told, and it is far from clear, what we are to understand by 'rhythm' in this sense. In the normal sense 'All movement is rhythmic' has a clear-enough meaning, which is well illustrated by the fact that we can produce counter-examples which refute the claim. But in the new sense it is no longer clear just what characteristic is being claimed for movement, and therefore how it could be confirmed or disconfirmed.

There are exceptions. H'Doubler (1946), for example, writes: 'Rhythm therefore may be defined as *force manifest in muscle action*.' This at least has the merit of stating clearly how the author intends to use the word (although I leave aside the question of whether in every case of movement there is force manifest in muscle action). However, its great demerit is that the word has been redefined in a way which removes it so far from its normal meaning that considerable confusion is likely to ensue. For 'force manifest in muscle action' has no relation at all to the accounts of the meaning of 'rhythm' which we considered earlier. As we shall see in Chapter 6, a definition must be substitutable, without change of meaning, for the term defined. For instance, 'bachelor' can be defined as 'unmarried man', thus, instead of saying 'I am a bachelor', I could substitute 'I am an unmarried man'. However, if we employ this test with H'Doubler's definition of 'rhythm' we generate some bizarre results. You may have heard the old jazz song 'I got rhythm'. It would hardly be the same to say 'I got force manifest in muscle action'.

Moreover, H'Doubler herself, not surprisingly, appears to have slipped back into something like the normal meaning when she says later in her book: 'Rhythm tends to cause movements to become automatic, facilitating execution.' It is difficult to see how force manifest in muscle action can facilitate execution by producing the economy of a 'grooved' action. But it is not at all difficult to appreciate that to develop a good rhythm, in the sense of an appropriate recurring pattern, can be of considerable help, indeed it may be indispensable, in the efficient execution of a range of movements, for example a tennis service and a golf swing.

A further consequence of insisting that all movement is rhythmic is the loss of a useful distinction. For if we accept the recurrent pattern sense, then there are efficient and inefficient rhythmic movements and *also* non-rhythmic movements.

The same problem occurs in music. Some people insist that there is rhythm in all music, and thus to talk of 'non-rhythmic music' would be considered as much a flat self-contradiction as to talk of a non-married husband. Yet some modern jazz solos, for example, are played deliberately to break right away from any rhythmic pattern. Similarly, at a conference on contemporary dance in 1975, Alwin Nikolais emphatically rejected that part of the Webster Dictionary definition of dance which asserts that it is 'rhythmic movement', and insisted, on the contrary: 'Movement does not have to be rhythmic *at all* to be dance.'

Another version of the meaning of the term is exemplified by Raffé (1964): 'Rhythm is not single . . . it must be integrated into an indivisible unity to attain irrefutable success.' Mettler (1942), too, seems to have something like this conception: 'Rhythm is the inner force which integrates and relates the parts of every whole to the whole and to each other.' This view of rhythm is the same as, or closely related to, the third *Concise Oxford Dictionary* account given above, of a harmonious correlation of parts, but there are insuperable difficulties about maintaining both this version and the thesis that there is rhythm in all movement. For not all movement is part of a harmonious whole, if of any whole, since there are many movements which are unrelated to anything else. Moreover, not all wholes, for example whole dance or athletic performances, would be agreed to be harmonious.

Some writers appear to use 'rhythmic' as the equivalent of 'well co-ordinated', 'smooth-flowing', 'well timed' or 'efficiently and economically directed', as in a good tennis service or golf swing. However, as most of us know to our cost, either as teachers or performers, not all movements are rhythmic in this sense, since there are so many actions in tennis and in golf, as in all other sporting events, which are certainly *not* well co-ordinated, smooth-flowing, well timed, or efficiently and economically directed to the requisite end.

Sometimes, particularly in dance, the word 'rhythm' seems to be used to refer to the whole structure of any complete performance, whether or not it is harmonious or well co-ordinated. But then either it would be illegitimate to speak, in the same sense, of the rhythm of any particular constituent movement, since it is not a complete performance in itself, or to say that there is rhythm in all the dance movements would amount to no more than saying that parts of the dance are parts of the dance. For since, according to this usage, the whole of every performance is necessarily rhythmic, it is also necessarily true that each constituent movement must be rhythmic.

Sometimes it is even implied or stated that all movement must be rhythmic because the whole universe is based on rhythm. Such claims differ from those discussed above in that they do not necessarily or exclusively accept the requirement of a recurring pattern, or appeal to physical theories about the nature of matter. Instead, they tend to appeal to some mysterious transcendental rhythmical quality which is supposed to be inherent in man, or even in all things, as a consequence of the movement of the heavenly bodies. For example, Haskell (1960) writes: 'Why should movements be rhythmical? The answer can be found in the universe around us and in ourselves.' Mettler (1942) makes a similar point: 'Rhythm . . . is universal. It functions in space as well as in time. Color, line, area and mass have rhythm, for behind each lies an organic motor impulse.' Later she writes: 'No simple movement can be lacking in rhythm since rhythm means the inner life of the movement . . . The human being can feel within his own body some of the ramifications of the cosmic pulse . . .' More startlingly, Meerloo (1962) states quite baldly: 'Everything is rhythm.' It is difficult to know what that statement could mean. In the normal sense, it seems absurd to suggest that this book, the desk on which I am writing, and my left sock are all rhythm. Moreover, quite apart from the dubious metaphysics of such arguments, it would follow that nothing which exists or occurs could *ever* be non-rhythmic, in which case there would appear to be little, if anything, in the claim that all movement is rhythmic. At least we require a convincing argument to explain what could be meant by such a claim. It appears, on the face of it, that this is another example of a confused slide from one sense of the term to another.

EXTENDED SENSE

Now I should like to return to my earlier point that a concept with a central meaning may develop an extended sense. This notion may help to explain the more unusual cases of the attribution of rhythm, and also how some of the writers quoted may have become confused. The point can be most clearly explained by examples. Consider the phrase —vv. It may occur only once, in sound, movement or a visual pattern, yet it may be seen as rhythmic by analogy with a waltz rhythm. Another example might be vvv—, which might be regarded as rhythmic in isolation, by anyone familiar with Beethoven's Fifth Symphony. It is here, I suggest, that we might find a clue to how the concept of rhythm may come to be extended to apply to *any* recognisable pattern. For example, in certain cases we speak of a tennis service action as rhythmic, and this is implicitly to relate this particular action to the presumed possibility of performing an exactly similar action again and again. It would, for instance, be very surprising, to say the least, if someone were able to produce a perfect cannonball service only once. This, I think, is why there is a tendency to use the term 'rhythmic' only of accomplished actions of this sort. We are less likely to speak of the action of a total beginner as rhythmic, because it is presumed that he cannot reproduce the same action again. This may also explain the tendency, often not consciously recognised, to regard the attribution of 'rhythmic' to movement as in some way positively evaluative, and 'non-rhythmic' as a criticism. So that to say that a dance or movement lacks rhythm is often taken to imply that it is of poor quality. An example which struck me recently was when a cricket commentator observed that the spin bowler, Derek Underwood, had 'recovered his rhythm', which meant that he was now able to bowl again with a confident, smooth action as a result of knowing that he could produce that action regularly.

Another way of explaining this extended sense is to say that the concept of rhythm may be employed internally or externally. An example of internal rhythm would be that of a poem, in which the poet establishes a rhythm for that particular work. That is, the rhythm is intrinsic, and can be recognised solely by an examination of that poem itself, independently of any other. On the other hand, the waltz or tango pattern of beats or sounds, occurring just once, or a single golf swing or tennis service action, would be rhythmic in an external sense, because of its implicit relation to a context *outside* itself in which there is or could be a recurrent pattern. That is, the movement, in this case, does not as does the poem, carry its own internal rhythm.

It is important, then, to recognise that the concept of rhythm can be applied very widely by extension or analogy. Yet we should beware of the temptation, to which so many writers succumb, of sliding from this into the belief that there is *no* movement in which some pattern of rhythm could not be perceived if only our powers of observation were sufficiently acute. For this in turn leads to a lot of metaphysical non-sense about peculiar powers of detection, or rhythm which is there but which cannot be detected. Hence the confusion of writers who make extravagant claims that rhythm is in all movement, or is the basis of the universe, science and art, or even, is everything. It is important to recognise that a term can coherently be employed in an extended sense only when it is possible to offer some grounds to justify such an extension.

Perhaps it is a failure to recognise this point which explains to some extent how writers on the topic can become so confused and confusing. For instance, Bruce (1970) writes: 'There is the rhythm of shape and space, in nature's forming, and in man's creativity.' It is difficult to understand what that means, and it is even more difficult to understand her quotation from Shelley: 'Rhythm is to intuition and emotion and aesthetics what scientific order and logic are to the intellect.' As far as I can understand it, this seems to be incompatible with her enthusiastic agreement with Dalcroze that rhythm is the basis of all science, mathematics and machinery.

Bruce also quotes Dalcroze approvingly as recognising that a lack of musical rhythm in a person is not so much a gap in musical awareness as an a-rhythmic condition of the whole being. Yet not only is this highly questionable, since someone with a poorly developed musical sense of rhythm might still have a well-developed sense of the rhythm of movement, but, more damagingly, it again involves her in self-contradiction, since she earlier states that 'We each have our personal rhythms . . .', and this presumably applies even to the person who lacks a sense of musical rhythm.

My tentative suggestion is, then, that Bruce and the other writers quoted are led to making such extravagant and inconsistent statements partly because of a failure to recognise the dangers of confusion inherent in using 'rhythm' in an extended sense. Up to a point it may continue to be illuminating, but these authors seem to have extended it beyond that point, so that the term becomes drained of intelligible substance.

CONCLUSION

As we have seen, it may be possible to consider a wide variety of phenomena as rhythmic in an extended sense, or by analogy with the central cases where there is a clear recurrent pattern, but that is certainly not to say that just anything can be usefully or intelligibly said to exhibit a rhythmic pattern. In such cases one needs to ask what is the *point* of applying the concept of rhythm, i.e. does it have any explanatory value? A universal application is not merely pointless, but actually harmful, since it is not only confusing but eliminates a distinction which is very useful for those concerned with human movement. In this sphere it is often very helpful to consider the rhythm of a movement. Indeed, it may be essential, on grounds of efficiency and economy of effort, to develop a rhythm in an action such as a tennis service, as many of us know to our cost, since the performance of the action is so difficult. It has to be grooved into an unconscious rhythm, so that it can be reproduced at will without conscious effort.

Nevertheless, it is clear that not all movements are of this kind, and, to repeat the point, not just anything can intelligibly be said to be rhythmic. The requirement of some sort of recurring pattern or the possibility of relating to such a pattern, may be a very humble necessary condition for the correct use of the term 'rhythm' and its cognates, but if even that should be abandoned it is hard to distinguish any residual basis of generally agreed meaning which could serve to stem the tide of continued confusion in the use of a term which is so frequently applied in a wide range of physical activities. Without such a basis we are in danger of losing a distinction which is very valuable to an understanding of human movement.

REFERENCES: CHAPTER 3

Bruce, V. R., *Movement in Silence and Sound* (London: Bell & Sons, 1970).
Haskell, A. L., *The Story of Dance* (London: Rathbone Books, 1960).
H'Doubler, M., 'Movement and Its Rhythmic Structure' (Madison, Wisconsin: mimeographed by Kramer Business Service, 1946).
Jordan, D., *Childhood and Movement* (Oxford: Basil Blackwell, 1966).

Meerloo, J. A. M., *Dance Craze and Sacred Dance* (London: Peter Owen, 1961).

Mettler, B., 'What is rhythm?', reprinted from *Educational Dance* in Mettler, *Nine Articles on Dance* (Boston, Mass.: Mettler Studios, 1942).

North, M., *An Introduction to Movement Study and Teaching* (London: Macdonald & Evans, 1971).

Preston, V., *A Handbook for Modern Educational Dance* (London: Macdonald & Evans, 1963).

Raffé, W. G., *Dictionary of Dance* (London: Thomas Yoseloff, 1964).

Russell, J., *Creative Dance in the Secondary School* (London: Macdonald & Evans, 1969).

Note

This section has been revised in the light of some interesting comments, for which I am very grateful, on an earlier draft of the paper, by some of my former colleagues at Chelsea School of Human Movement. I am especially indebted, for some perceptive suggestions, to Ralph Homer.

Chapter 4

Movement and the Intellect

INTRODUCTION

Writing and discussion on the contribution made by the practical performance of the activities which comprise sport and physical
education to the development of the intellect frequently reveal two
common and usually closely related misconceptions. These are to
assume (1) that 'the intellect' is equivalent to 'the mental', and refers
to some general capacity for thinking, and (2) that the intellect is a
distinct, inner faculty which causes thoughtful actions, i.e. this is part
of a dualist conception of the body and mind as separate entities.
Although they are not necessarily related, in practice they are usually
to be found in conjunction, since the former misconception leads
naturally to the latter. Consequently I shall concentrate primarily on
the former.

It is important to eradicate the confusion on this issue not only for
the sake of clarity *per se* but also because of the practical damage
which it can effect in the discussion and formulation of degree
proposals in human-movement studies.

THE DEVELOPMENT OF THE INTELLECT

Statements are often made which explicitly claim, imply or at least are
commonly taken to imply, that the activities which comprise sport,
and physical education or human movement contribute to the
development of the intellect. Such a conclusion is also frequently
taken to be implied by claims made about 'education *through* movement'. For expository purposes let us consider how this conclusion is
reached with respect to Modern Educational Gymnastics, since the
argument for it brings out clearly one of the major but erroneous
assumptions to which I want to draw attention. However, I should
like to emphasise that similar claims are made with respect to other
activities in physical education and sport. It is said, then, that Modern
Educational Gymnastics develops, stimulates, or in some other way
improves, the intellect. The argument for the claim goes something
like this:

> Modern Educational Gymnastics requires more thought than
> formal gymnastics, since there is an indefinitely wide possibility of

choice of method in answering the tasks. Hence the participants have to think out for themselves the best ways of answering each task, and since there is more thinking involved, a greater contribution is made to intellectual development.

The misconception inherent in this sort of argument is the former of those mentioned above, namely that of an oversimple notion of the intellect as a *general* mental faculty which can be developed and exercised in various ways, just as muscles can be developed by means of various physical exercises. Such a misconception is implicit, for example, in Morgan *et al.* (1970), who write of the power of a well-conceived programme of physical activity to 'exercise the intellect' and 'influence the minds as well as the bodies' of pupils. Jean Williams (1974) seems to have a similar conception, since she quotes with approval one of the aims of physical education stated by Morgan *et al.*, as 'Intellectual . . . development through physical activities'. In a similar vein, Morgan (1974) writes of 'a range of activities, some of them highly organised and socially sophisticated, appealing often to the intellect as well as to the centres of motor control'. A classic case of this misapprehension can be seen in Chapter 3 of Arnold's book (1968), significantly entitled 'The Mental *Element*' (my italics). For example, of play activities Arnold writes: 'The "prepared environment" with its water, sand, clay, blocks and open spaces positively enhances sensory and other forms of experiences so that the intelligence and intellect become nourished from the richness of the surroundings.'

But it is misleading to conceive of the intellect in terms of a general faculty which can be 'nourished', since the assumption on which it depends, that there is an essential homogeneity in or underlying all types of thinking, is manifestly false. For the terms 'thinking' and 'mental' cover a heterogeneous range of cases. Metheny (1965) fails to recognise the importance of this point, and it has damaging consequences for her theory. Among other examples in her book, one finds: 'In human life as we know it, thought and behaviour are the two sides of the coin of human existence. Each implies the other; neither can exist apart from the other. Thus, man has no choice other than "to express his thoughts" in behavioural form.' From this sort of consideration she concludes: 'We may therefore say with some confidence that voluntary movement experiences have intellectual content.' Similarly, Morgan (1974) writes: 'All actions will be, in some measure or other, in subservience to the intellect and the will. Much education will be effected through the conscious activation of the intellectual powers through comprehension and value judgment.'

Now certainly there is an important difference between a 'mindless' movement, such as a reflex action, and an intentional action, and it is true that voluntary action is intentional. A way of expressing this might be to say that voluntary action is thought-impregnated. But there is great diversity in *kinds* of thinking, and only confusion can accrue from assimilating them all to some supposedly unified mental faculty called 'the intellect'. One can be said to be thinking when daydreaming about winning the football pools, wondering where to go on holiday, wishing one could stay in bed on a cold morning, and admiring beautiful scenery. Moreover, one may be thinking what one is doing when performing the voluntary movements involved in sweeping the floor, reversing a car through a narrow gateway, and picking a chicken bone. Yet it would sound very odd to call any of these activities 'intellectual', or to suggest that they have 'intellectual content', or that they are performed 'in subservience to the intellect'. Furthermore, although it is true that comprehension and the making of value-judgements require thought, they certainly do not necessarily or even usually require *intellectual* thought. For instance, learning to ride a bicycle involves comprehension, and deciding which of two cars to buy usually involves a value-judgement, but neither is an intellectual activity, even although both may demand considerable thought.

To write of voluntary movement as having intellectual content, or to write of all (intentional) actions as being in subservience to the intellect clearly reveals that Metheny and Morgan, respectively, conceive of the intellect as a unified faculty of general thinking. Yet, as Wittgenstein (1967) points out:

> 'Thinking' is a widely ramified concept. A concept that comprises many manifestations of life. The *phenomena* of thinking are widely scattered . . . It is not to be expected of this word that it should have a unified employment; we should rather expect the opposite.

Whereas it is true that when one is performing an intellectual activity one is necessarily thinking, it is not true that when one is thinking one is necessarily performing an intellectual activity. That is, 'intellectual' entails 'thinking', but the converse does not hold, i.e. 'thinking' does not entail 'intellectual'. The old country yokel who, asked what he did on summer evenings, replied: 'Sometimes I sits and thinks, and sometimes I just sits', would be startled to hear that therefore he is sometimes an intellectual.

Another source of confusion which is part of the same misconception is clearly exemplified in Arnold's book (1968): 'The intelligence of a person is closely associated with his intellectual abilities'; 'it becomes hard to see how early physical activity can fail to contribute towards the growth of overall intelligence and *thus* to overall intellectual functioning'; and 'play may be said to further if not foster the growth of intelligence and *thus* make a contribution to the child's intellectual advancement' (my italics). One can, of course, perform gymnastics, sporting activities generally, and indeed, most physical activities *intelligently*, but that is certainly not to say that *ipso facto* one is being *intellectual*. Indeed, we often speak of animals as intelligent, but not as intellectual. In short, 'intelligent' does not entail 'intellectual', and failure to recognise this leads to the sort of confusion exemplified by Arnold.

THE INTELLECT AS AN INNER FACULTY

The misconception considered above, of regarding the intellect as a unified mental faculty, is commonly, in practice, related to another widespread misconception, namely that of construing the intellect as an *inner* faculty, quite separate from observable behaviour. Such a notion is a manifestation of a dualist conception of body and mind, i.e. it construes them as logically distinct entities which are only causally related. We shall consider below one of the problems encountered by the notion that the intellect determines, in this way, intentional action, but for the present let us try to see how understandable it is to relate both misconceptions. If one assumes 'the intellect' to refer to every kind of thinking it is also natural to assume that it refers to the *source* of all thoughtful activity, and this gives a picture of some sort of *inner* source which causes or determines all thinking and thoughtful activity.

A factor which largely contributes to this misconception is what might be called the 'naming' theory of meaning. There is a strong tendency to assume that a substantive must refer to a substance, i.e. that a noun must refer to an object or entity of some sort. Thus 'the table' refers to a locatable table, 'the President' refers to a locatable person, and hence it is natural to assume that the singular term 'the intellect' must also refer to something, and, since it cannot be spatially located, that it must exist as an unperceivable mental entity. To write of the mind or intellect as a 'component' or an 'element' which can be 'nourished', especially in the context of the respective books, certainly appears to reflect the conception of such an inner faculty. And there can hardly be any other interpretation of writing of all action as 'in subservience' to the intellect.

But such a theory of mind can be reduced to incoherence for reasons precisely similar to those adduced against the ideationist theory of meaning which was considered in Chapter 1. For the epistemological question, 'How is it possible to know?' reveals the impossibility, even in principle, of discovering whether such an inner entity could be the cause of thoughtful or intentional action, or even whether such an entity could be said to exist. That is, according to the theory itself there is no possibility of confirming or disconfirming the existence, let alone the causal effects, of 'the intellect', construed in this way, hence the theory reduces to unintelligibility. To put the point another way, construed as an inner faculty about which nothing could possibly be known to observers, the notion of the intellect can serve no explanatory purpose. Our concern will be solely with whether, for instance, a child gets his sums right, and any question of the possible existence and influence of such an inaccessible entity can be of no concern or relevance. It could certainly add nothing to our understanding of thoughtful, intelligent or intentional action.

Yet this is a very common misconception, so it is important to be aware of it, and how easy it is to slip into it. For there is a great temptation to assume that an action is *thoughtful* because it is endowed with the requisite quality by an underlying, inner mental faculty. Wittgenstein (1967) locates the temptation perfectly: 'One imagines thinking as the stream which must be flowing under the surface of these expedients if they are not after all to be mere mechanical procedures.' Yet, as we have seen, no sense can be made of the notion of an unobservable inner mental faculty which can be exercised in various observable activities. It is not that the mind or intellect suffuses the activity with thoughtful quality, but rather that the activity in question simply *is* one of the many kinds which are thoughtful. To put the point another way, no sense can be given to the notion of an inner faculty of the intellect which endows an activity with intellectual quality. On the contrary, we need to consider the activity *itself* to determine whether it is of the kind which is called 'intellectual'.

This kind of misapprehension can be avoided by recognising that 'the intellect' cannot coherently be regarded as alluding to some inner faculty which makes possible the relevant forms of activity, but is a convenient shorthand for alluding to a person's capacity for dealing with some of the various *activities* which are called 'intellectual'. Nevertheless, one should beware of the seductive tendency to misconception implicit in the use of the singular term 'the intellect'.

THE INTELLECT – DETERMINED BY INTELLECTUAL ACTIVITIES

This raises the question of what it is to be intellectual. It is not necessary even if it were possible usefully to conduct a full-scale analysis, but we can obtain a rough idea of the distinction marked by the term, and that is sufficient for our purposes. There are some activities, such as mathematics, the pure sciences, and philosophy, which are incontrovertibly intellectual. There are others, such as cutting the hedge, playing snakes and ladders, going for a walk, and engaging in social chat, which are clearly not intellectual. Ryle (1949) writes:

> When we speak of the intellect, or better, of the intellectual powers and performances of persons, we are referring primarily to that special class of operations which constitute theorising. The goal of the operations is the knowledge of true propositions or facts. Mathematics and the established natural sciences are the model accomplishments of human intellects.

However, not all theorising would count as intellectual. A discussion of tennis or squash tactics, for example, might be regarded as theoretical, but not normally as intellectual. The term tends to be restricted to those activities which involve a fairly considerable degree of high-level theorising or abstraction. When, as undergraduates, we went rowing at university, it was partly as a relaxation from intellectual pursuits. Rowing, like many sports, requires considerable thought and concentration, but we certainly would not have engaged in it, after a day of examinations for instance, if it had been yet more *intellectual* activity.

This begins to reveal just how fundamental is the error implicit in the common supposition, exemplified by Arnold and the other authors quoted, that the intellect is some sort of mental faculty which is the underlying source of and is manifest in all thinking and thoughtful action. Such an erroneous conception is part of the pervasive myth in the literature on physical education of what is often vaguely called 'the body/mind dichotomy', or of the tripartite division of the human personality into 'thinking, feeling and doing' aspects—sometimes more pretentiously formulated in terms of 'cognitive, affective and conative' domains—with the *de fide* assumption that physical education activities can provide the desired 'synthesis', 'unity of the organism', 'wholeness' or 'integration'. (It is significant that these and similar terms, such as 'holism', occur so frequently in the writing of Arnold and others on this theme.) Phenix (1964) exhibits the same error:

> A person cannot think without a body, nor are his motor responses independent of thought. If learning is to be organic, provision needs to be made for activities in which the intellectual and motor *components* of experience are deliberately correlated. This union of thought, feeling, sense and act is the particular aim of the arts of

movement and of the fields of health, recreation, and physical education. Nowhere else is the co-ordination of all *components* of the living person so directly fostered. (my italics)

It is ironic that such authors tend strenuously to deny that their work clearly reveals an underlying and incoherent preconception of a divided personality, or dualist theory of mind, since it is this very conception to which they believe they are explicitly opposed in advancing their arguments in support of the value of physical education. Yet the irony is that the very formulation of their argument in those terms itself manifests precisely that misconception, since they inevitably have to presuppose separate entities or domains in order to argue that the supposedly desired 'wholeness' or 'integration' can be achieved, for instance by *thoughtful* physical activity. It is precisely this 'synthesising' function to which Arnold appeals, supposing it to be the principal strength of his case. The notion is that there are two or three elements, components or domains of a person which can be united if an adequate programme of physical education is devised. Thus it is assumed that the provision of physical activity which also requires thought will 'synthesise' or 'integrate' the physical and the intellectual, producing 'wholeness' or 'the unity of the organism', or, as a special bonus, 'holism'. By providing also for the affective, for example through the opportunity for emotional expression in dance, it is supposed that all three aspects of a person can be brought together.

What fatally undermines Arnold's argument is the underlying implicit assumption, which he is unable to recognise, of distinct and separable domains of the personality. In short, the whole enterprise of trying to produce an argument of this sort, which is all too common in the literature on physical education, is hopelessly vitiated from the start by the presupposition of a grossly oversimplified concept of mind which, for good reasons, has long been outmoded in philosophy. For even the most cursory examination reveals the inadequacy of the conception on which this whole line of argument depends. For example, which is the appropriate domain for the activity in which I am engaged as I write these words—thinking, feeling or doing? 'Thinking' may seem the obvious answer. Yet I am also *doing* philosophy, and I am involved in the physical activity of writing. Moreover, I often *feel* dissatisfied or depressed, and less often satisfied or even pleased, by my work. So, on a parity of reasoning, am I entitled to regard philosophy as holistic, since it produces a unity of my organism?

As we have seen above, Morgan (1974) conceives of all actions as 'in some measure or other, in *subservience* to the intellect and the will' (my italics). Implicit in this quotation there resides not only the misconception of regarding the intellect as the faculty which is the source of thinking in general, but also another commonly encountered misconception. Notice that all actions are said to be 'in subservience' to the intellect and the will, which clearly implies that every voluntary action is ordained by preceding thought and a consequent decision to act. Presumably the sequence of events is supposed to be rather as follows: I think about a possible action with my intellect, and when I have decided to carry it out my will puts the decision into effect, and thus a voluntary action is performed. It is commonly assumed that only in this way can voluntary action be distinguished from involuntary action, since the latter may be, in purely physical respects, identical with the former. That is, the only way to account for the voluntary or intentional nature of an action is assumed to be in terms of its being ordained by previous thought and volition. Thus the assumption is that voluntary action is to be explained in the following way: first the intellect formulates the decision to act, and then the will ensures that the action is carried out.

This sort of explanation of action may seem plausible at first sight, yet it can quickly be shown to be no genuine explanation at all. It is supposed that each voluntary action occurs as a result of a prior intellectual decision. But that intellectual decision is itself a voluntary action, thus it also requires a prior intellectual decision. But that intellectual decision is itself a voluntary action, thus it also requires a prior intellectual decision. But that intellectual decision is itself a voluntary action, and so on *ad infinitum*. In short, the supposition that all action is in subservience to or ordained by the intellect and the will reduces to what is called in philosophy a 'vicious infinite regress', which is a *reductio ad absurdum*, i.e. a method of demonstrating the incoherence of the supposition by spelling out its consequences. For in a vicious infinite regress it is shown that the regress has to be completed before the initial explanation can be offered. Yet, because the regress is infinite, it can obviously never be completed, hence one is unable even to *begin* on the explanation, since one first requires what is to be explained in order to explain what is required. Roughly, it is like trying to give an answer to the question, 'Which came first, the chicken or the egg?'

Now it seems quite clear that to speak of all actions as 'in subservience to the intellect and will' carries the implication considered above, i.e. the misconception of assuming them to be inner faculties which causally determine intentional or voluntary action. It is hard to know what other construction could be put on such a use of the terms. But if, somewhat implausibly, it should be contended that no such implication was intended, and that this formulation is simply a picturesque way of referring to intentional or voluntary action, then such a defence would incur an embarrassing consequence. For first one would want to know why such an eccentric and misleading characterisation of action is offered, and secondly, if that is all that is intended, it provides not even a superficial attempt at *explanation* of such action, but only an oddly idiosyncratic alternative way of referring to it. For to talk of it as 'in subservience to the intellect and will' can then amount to no more than saying that a voluntary action is one which we decide to perform. Thus to write of action as in subservience to the intellect and will is either to conceive of them as inner faculties—in which case an explanation of action is offered, but it is vulnerable to the argument adduced above—or to offer no explanation at all of action.

EVALUATIVE CONTENT

Another factor which exacerbates the confusion on this issue is that 'intellectual' tends to be used evaluatively, hence to confess that an activity, especially in higher education, is not intellectual seems to denigrate it. This, I think, partly explains the motivation of those who, because they want to argue that physical-education activities are no less valuable in education than some academic subjects, feel that consequently they have to try to prove that engaging in such physical activities *does* involve the intellect. In this respect, I have heard it argued that it would be legitimate to use the term 'kinaesthetic intellect', and that we should not restrict 'intellectual' to purely cognitive activities. But this is a confusion, since to speak of a 'non-cognitive intellectual activity' sounds very much like a contradiction in terms. Perhaps a case could be made for the use of the term *'kinaesthetic intelligence'* if this were to mean, for example, the ability to perform a variety of physical actions skilfully and to overcome new problems in different situations with dexterity and imagination etc. In Modern Educational Gymnastics, for instance, students are encouraged not only to extend their physical capacity to perform a greater diversity of movements, but also to develop an increasing ingenuity in answering a variety of tasks. There might well be some point in describing an able performer here as exhibiting kinaesthetic intelligence. But to put my earlier point another way, the able mover who is not intellectually gifted will perform physical activities more competently, will exhibit greater kinaesthetic intelligence, than the intellectually gifted who is not an able mover.

It has been objected against my argument that to use 'intellectual' to apply only to the sorts of activities I have mentioned, and to refuse to apply it to physical-education activities is mere academic prejudice. The objector claimed that in some Eastern countries the subjects are divided up in different ways, and that our method of classification is simply a Western convention. There are some deep philosophical confusions which underlie this objection, but it is not necessary to pursue them fully in order to refute it. Notice, first, that the objector cannot have it *both* ways. He cannot consistently argue *both* that 'intellectual' is used arbitrarily, since it depends solely on Western conventions and academic prejudice, *and* that physical-education activities are intellectual. The objection clearly reveals his own evaluative notion of 'intellectual' in this confused argument.

More importantly, if the objection amounts to the claim that we use the term 'intellectual' to apply to certain activities, such as mathematics, when we could have used another term, or the same term to mark a different distinction, then of course this is true. But it will not help the objector, for if we widen the term to include physical activities then we shall have blurred or eradicated a useful distinction, and we shall have to provide another term to refer to activities such as mathematics, philosophy and the sciences. The division is not arbitrary, even though a different term could be used to mark it, and even though various kinds of division are possible. For if in a different society gymnastics and mathematics went more naturally together than philosophy and mathematics, this would raise serious doubts about whether 'gymnastics' meant the same as it does in our society. We might expect to find, for example, that what they call 'gymnastics' is a sort of active chess, and thus in important respects very different from our gymnastics. On the other hand, if we were to discover that 'gymnastics' did mean the same as in our society yet it was still called an 'intellectual' activity, it would be clear that in that society 'intellectual' does not mean what it does in ours. Perhaps the point can be more clearly brought out in this way. It largely constitutes the *meaning* of the term 'intellectual' that it is used to distinguish those activities which are properly described as 'intellectual' from physical activities such as sport. This brings up another objection to those who, like Morgan *et al.* (1970), quoted above, believe that a well-conceived programme of physical activity can 'exercise the intellect' as well as the body. Even if 'the intellect' is construed as shorthand for 'intellectual abilities', the assertion is still confused. For when *performing* the activities of even an enlightened physical-education programme, pupils are certainly not engaged in *intellectual* activities. That is, by virtue of its *meaning*, the term 'intellectual' is properly used to mark the *contradistinction* from such physical activities.

Referring back to the point adduced above, concerning the evaluative content of 'intellectual', it can now be seen that one would be on much safer ground readily to concede that physical-education activities are not intellectual, but to argue that they are none the less valuable for that.

THE CONTRIBUTION OF THE INTELLECTUAL

Now it is of the first importance that my argument should not be misconstrued. I am certainly *not* saying that it is impossible to be intellectual about physical-education activities. On the contrary, I should want to insist that it is not only possible but necessary, for a more comprehensive understanding of them, to consider such activities from the points of view of the disciplines of, for example, physiology, psychology, sociology and philosophy. What I *am* arguing is that in *performing* physical activities, even thoughtfully, one is not, or at least is not normally and necessarily, engaged in intellectual activities. By contrast, to engage thoughtfully in, for example, higher mathematics, *is* necessarily to engage in an intellectual activity. To fail to understand this point could have a damaging effect on the formulation of proposals for degree courses in human movement in which intellectual content is demanded. Such a failure stems from a fundamentally misconceived oversimplification of, and therefore confusion about, mental concepts, to which it is the principal concern of this chapter to draw attention.

CONCEPTUAL ABILITIES

One further misconception which exacerbates the confusion is bound up with a very loose usage of the term 'concept' and its cognates. The term 'conceptualisation', for example, is often misleadingly employed—not only in debate about physical education but also, for instance, in educational theory and psychology—to refer to any sort of knowledge. We briefly considered the use of the term 'concept' and its cognates in Chapter 1, but further elucidation is required here. The principal point for our present purposes can be illustrated in this way: it is quite possible to be able to swim without having any understanding of the concept of swimming, and conversely to understand the concept of swimming without being able to swim.

Now this contention has been received with a mixture of dismay and hostility by some physical educationists on both sides of the Atlantic, yet such a reaction stems largely from a failure to understand precisely what I mean by the notion of a concept. The grasp of a concept, as we saw in Chapter 1, is a matter of the mastery of language, of understanding logical implications and connections. Thus, for example, both a seal and a fish can swim far more competently than any human being, yet it would be absurd to suggest that either could have any grasp of the *concept* of swimming, for which linguistic ability is necessary. Admittedly there may not be much point in employing concept-terminology in the case of swimming, but nevertheless there are ways in which a failure to understand the concept could be revealed. For instance, to speak of swimming on dry land, or in the air, if we exclude picturesque or other special uses of the term, would indicate such a failure. There is no way in which a seal or a fish could manifest conceptual ability or inability.

Presumably, the uneasiness felt by some physical educationists about the contention stems partly from the point made above concerning the evaluative implications of such terms as 'intellectual' and 'conceptual', and partly from the assumption that to deny that *conceptual* understanding is conferred by practical experience or expertise in an activity such as swimming is somehow to deny that *any* understanding is involved here. Yet one certainly would not wish to deny that good teaching can considerably improve understanding of *how* to swim. My point is that we should be careful to distinguish such understanding of practical performance from conceptual understanding.

There is a pervasive misconception about the experience of performing an activity, and the acquisition of conceptual understanding. It is often assumed that practical experience necessarily confers, or at least confers advantages in acquiring, conceptual understanding. Thus, the objection has been made that my example of the seal or fish is irrelevant to the human situation, since where a language-user is concerned the practical experience of swimming must have some beneficial effect on his ability to conceptualise. I would deny the irrelevance of the example, since it at least clearly reveals that practical expertise does not necessarily confer any conceptual grasp. But let us waive that point for the moment, and adduce another example to clarify the issue. Consider the question: Can a man who has been blind from birth have any grasp of the concept of colour? Probably as a result of the common underlying misconception, which was examined in Chapter 1, that a concept is an idea or image, there is a strong temptation to assume that necessarily he cannot, since he can have no experience of seeing colours. Yet this answer is not as obviously correct as it seems, and, indeed, it reveals at least an oversimplification, and probably a confusion, of the relevant issues. For a blind man can certainly correctly carry out various operations with colour words, and he would be able, for instance, to recognise inconsistencies in the ways people use such words. Thus, unlike an animal with perfect sight, he could certainly have a somewhat attenuated concept of colour. Moreover, he could be shown to have an understanding of the concept which was superior to that of a person with perfect sight but who was retarded educationally.

It is true that the blind man could not have as complete a grasp of colour concepts as most people who have the experience of seeing colours. But it is important to recognise that this is solely because there are various uses of the relevant *linguistic terms* which would be beyond his capacity. By contrast, and this is the point of the example, there is no superior ability in the employment of the term 'swimming' and its cognates which is necessarily conferred on the expert swimmer as a result of his practical experience, and which gives him advantages over those who cannot swim.

To take another example which involves a more legitimate employment of the term 'concept', however expertly a dancer or gymnast may be able to move in space, this ability does not necessarily imply that he has a competent grasp of the concept of space. A physically inactive philosopher who has carefully considered such questions as, 'Could there be a two-dimensional space?' is much more likely to have a comprehensive grasp of the concept. Understanding concepts at this level is a genuine intellectual enterprise. It is a matter of tracing out logical consequences, relations and possibilities. Of course, this is not to deny that a young child may be helped to begin to develop a rudimentary concept of space by moving, but it *is* to deny that at a later age he will necessarily or even usually continue to learn more about the concept in that way. But this is, in any case, an empirical, not a philosophical matter, which would presumably fall within the province of educational psychology. That is, to determine whether and at what ages practical experience of moving may contribute to conceptual understanding of space is a matter not for philosophical reasoning, but for experiment and observation.

A MATTER OF DEGREE

It has, perhaps, already become apparent from earlier discussion that the understanding of a concept is not a case of all-or-nothing, it is not that one either has grasped it or has failed to grasp it, but is rather a matter of degree. The importance of this point to the issue under consideration can be brought out by reference to a quotation from Ryle (1949) who writes:

> It is easy to see that intellectual development is a condition of the existence of all but the most primitive occupations and interests. Every advanced craft, game, project, amusement, organisation or industry is necessarily above the heads of untutored savages and infants, or else we would not call it 'advanced'. We do not have to be scientists in order to solve anagrams or play whist. But we have to be literate and be able to add and subtract.

This quotation might seem to support the claim that physical-education activities are intellectual after all. However, it should be noticed that Ryle here uses a very minimal sense of 'intellectual' such that it is a condition of 'all but the most primitive occupations'. Thus the term 'intellectual' in this sense marks off those actions which only a rational being can perform. But we should be clear (1) that this sense *does* imply only a minimal degree of the sort of ability we call 'intellectual', and (2) that therefore the term would not normally be used of such cases. No sharp distinction can be drawn here, but we would certainly want to deny that the term 'intellectual' would be legitimately employed to refer to activities which were only marginally above the capacity of untutored savages and infants. Higher mathematicians are notoriously inept at simple arithmetic, but we still regard them as intellectuals. We do not similarly call someone 'intellectual' who can do simple arithmetic but not, for example, higher mathematics.

The importance of this point emerges clearly in relation to a further attempt to defend the notion of intellectual development through physical activities. It has been objected against my argument that there must be a certain degree of the intellectual, even though it may be small, in performing sporting and other activities of the physical-education programme since they require at least some conceptual ability. My reply was that we refer to an activity as 'intellectual' only if it involves a considerable degree of that sort of thinking. If even this minimal sense were sufficient to justify calling an activity, 'intellectual', then it would be possible, on parity of reasoning, to propose a converse argument against the objector. One could claim that there is no need for physical education because we have enough physical exercise doing our intellectual activities. Philosophy, one could claim, is a physical activity, or nourishes the physique, since it involves the physiological functioning of the eyes and brain when reading, the ears and tongue when discussing, the limbs when walking to and from the library, and so on. Thus, on parity of argument, I could claim that philosophy develops the physical through the intellectual.

And if you'll swallow that, you'll swallow anything.

REFERENCES: CHAPTER 4

Arnold, P. J., *Education, Physical Education and Personality Development* (London: Heinemann, 1968).
Metheny, Eleanor, *Connotations of Movement in Sport and Dance* (Dubuque, Iowa: Wm C. Brown, 1965).
Morgan, R. E. *et al.*, 'The concept of physical education', *British Journal of Physical Education*, vol. 1, no. 4 (July 1970).

Morgan, R. E., *Concerns and Values in Physical Education* (London: Bell & Sons, 1974).

Phenix, P., *Realms of Meaning*, Chapter 14 (New York: McGraw-Hill, 1964).

Ryle, G., *The Concept of Mind* (London: Hutchinson, 1949).

Williams, Jean, *Themes for Educational Gymnastics* (London: Lepus Books, Henry Kimpton Publishers, 1974).

Wittgenstein, L., *Zettel* (Oxford: Basil Blackwell, 1967).

Chapter 5

The Empirical and the Conceptual

INTRODUCTION

In Chapter 1 a distinction was drawn between the empirical or scientific, and the logical or conceptual or philosophical, and it was pointed out that there is an interdependent relationship between these two modes of inquiry. Very often it is difficult to recognise when an empirical investigation involves conceptual considerations, hence a scientific examination may be conducted or attempted in a quite inappropriate sphere. Moreover, a failure to appreciate the importance of conceptual issues in general may lead to the common misapprehension that only mathematics and the sciences are capable of producing objective, factual conclusions, and therefore that any genuine claim to knowledge must be answerable to these disciplines. In relation to our sphere of interest, the assumption is that only empirical observation and experiment, along with the calculations based on them, can provide any justifiable support for statements made about human movement.

In this chapter it will be shown that there are important aspects of human behaviour which are outside the province of empirical investigation, but which can nevertheless be objectively substantiated. Indeed, contrary to what is commonly supposed, scientific verification itself inevitably presupposes theoretical issues.

'EMPIRICAL' AND 'CONCEPTUAL'

In Chapter 1 explanations were given of the terms 'empirical' and 'conceptual', but further clarification is required before we can adequately consider the issues to be raised in this chapter, since both terms are commonly used in ways which may be confusing.

I shall use the term 'empirical' in the way outlined in Chapter 1, such that empirical substantiation would be provided by 'going and seeing', i.e. by investigation. Thus the scientific is a more formal and rigorous sub-section of the empirical. The conceptual also involves discovering more about the world, but not by investigation, where this implies the collection of additional information. Conceptual understanding is given by considering the character or meaning of the information one already has. There may be an illuminating parallel here, in that just as the scientific is the more rigorous and systematic form of the empirical, so the philosophical is the more rigorous and systematic form of the conceptual. But there are numerous ways of increasing conceptual understanding which are not philosophical. Such understanding is revealed in the capacity to judge the character of people, for instance in a grasp of the various ways in which jealousy or sadness may be manifested. It is possible to go on increasing one's conceptual understanding of such matters indefinitely, as one increasingly learns to recognise the significance, for instance, of subtleties of facial expressions. Such understanding does not require further information, hence empirical investigation would be irrelevant. Someone with an inadequate grasp of the relevant concepts lacks the ability to recognise the significance of what is already before him. Similarly, an understanding of conceptual issues in morality may be shown in numerous non-philosophical ways, for instance as one becomes increasingly aware of the complexity involved in behaving sincerely. Understanding of both the character of people and morality can be increased through the arts. Again, although such under-standing is conceptual, it is not philosophical.

However, it is of the first importance to recognise that the conceptual in either sense is still answerable to *objective* features of the situation. For instance, one's judgement of a person's character depends upon how he actually *behaves*. Thus, in the sense in which I am using the terms, it is important to distinguish between the objective and the empirical. Both the conceptual and the empirical are objective, in that substantiation is given by what actually occurs or exists, but the conceptual is not empirical since, to repeat the point, no additional investigation or information is required.

The scientific and the philosophical are not concerned with *particular* cases in the same sense as the wider notions of the empirical and the conceptual respectively. The latter would be more concerned, for instance, with the concept of jealousy as it applies to a particular man, or with a particular moral judgement, whereas a philosophical concern, although still answerable to what *happens* objectively in the world, would be more general.

It is important, too, to recognise that in neither the empirical nor the conceptual case should one regard the more rigorous scientific or philosophical method, respectively, as *superior*. Often simply going to see whether there are mushrooms in the field, or simply forming an opinion of a person's behaviour, *without* precise measurement or rigorous philosophical analysis is *just* what is required.

OBJECTIVE POINTS OF VIEW

Let us first consider this issue in relation to the notion of aesthetic judgements about human movement, since it brings out clearly the point I wish to make. When one speaks of the beauty of the movements of, for instance, a pole-vaulter, a gymnast or a skater, it is not obvious how such statements could be supported by scientific investigation. Hence those imbued with the preconception that only the sciences can provide genuine knowledge assume that either some form of scientific justification must be discoverable, or that statements about the aesthetic quality of human movement are merely subjective, and thus that the notion of knowledge in this sphere is unintelligible.

A clear example of this sort of attitude can be found in an article by Spencer and White (1972), who complain that there are many vague claims made for the value of dance, and they suggest that these claims should be subjected to rigorous empirical, by which they clearly mean 'scientific', examination. They are suspicious of the dearth of empirical research in this field, since they assume that only scientific verification can substantiate what is said about dance. Moreover, it is clear from their article that they regard scientific examination as the only way in which any statement made about any form of human movement may be verified or refuted.

It should be noticed that the authors use the term 'phenomenon' in a significant and tendentious way. This is a term which can lead to some grave misconceptions, as we shall see in this chapter and the next. Spencer and White write of a lack of empirical investigation into dance 'as a phenomenon', and later they say that the use of 'diverse terms for what appear to be the same phenomenon' exacerbates the problem of empirical investigation. This is a classic case of the sort of confusion which can be engendered by an uncritical use of the term. For what is meant by 'phenomenon' in this context? Later in their article the authors show that they are aware that dance may be considered 'from various frames of reference', but from what frame of reference does one consider dance as a phenomenon? In order to consider anything it is necessary to know under what category or in which context it is to be considered. Usually, of course, this is implicit yet clearly understood. For example, if I were to ask you 'What do you think of this rose?', you would be unlikely to consider its merits as a paperweight. You would, under normal circumstances, consider it in relation to other roses or flowers. Similarly, if I were to ask your opinion of a piece of sculpture, you would normally assume that an aesthetic judgement would be the appropriate kind of response, and you would be surprised if it were to be evaluated as a doorstop. However, in some cases it may be necessary to make explicit the category under which the object is to be considered. For example, when your opinion is sought of an old armchair, you might have to ask, 'Do you mean from the point of view of comfort or appearance?'

The relevance of this issue can be brought out in this way. Suppose that apropos of nothing in particular I show you an ordinary twig, and say 'What do you think of that?' You will be at a complete loss to know how to answer me, because nothing in the context has given you an indication of the category under which I want you to consider it. Your puzzlement is unlikely to be resolved if I add: 'I mean, what do you think of it as a phenomenon?' Similarly, it is necessary to know under which category one is supposed to be considering dance before any comment can be offered as to the possibility of fruitfully conducting an empirical investigation and as to the form which such an investigation should take. Consequently, there is a good reason why we need at least *some* 'diverse terms for what appear to be the same phenomenon', since different terms will be required in order to indicate the different categories under which dance can be considered.

Now, it is a clear presupposition in Spencer and White's article that there is no doubt about the kind of category under which we are to consider the phenomenon of dance, which is why I said that their use of the term 'phenomenon' was both tendentious and significant. Given the general tenor of their argument, it is apparent that they intend us to consider movement from the points of view of such empirical sciences as physiology, kinesiology, biomechanics and biochemistry. But although one should be sceptical of the rapturous and sibylline phraseology which so often characterises the literature on dance, it is important to understand why terms other than scientific ones are required. For the interests of many of the authors quoted in their article are wholly, or at least predominantly, in dance *as an art form*, and that is not the same as an interest in dance from the point of view of one of the empirical sciences. Hence different terms are required in order to mark this different kind of interest. Moreover, it certainly cannot be assumed that because statements about movement are made which are not open to scientific verification they are *ipso facto* not open to any sort of objective substantiation. Not all objective kinds of interest are scientific, as we shall see.

There may be another way in which the use of 'phenomenon' is significant. It may be that Spencer and White are aware to some extent of the conceptual problem about differences of categories of interest. Hence, perhaps they want to use the term as a generic one, to cover the various kinds of ways in which movement can be considered. That is, 'phenomenon' is to operate neutrally across the boundaries of the different categories under which movement can be subsumed. It seems to me that this notion underlies, and in my opinion vitiates, a good deal of literature on the phenomenology of movement, as we shall see in the next chapter. For, as will be clear from the example given above, such a notion is unintelligible. It would be equivalent to my asking you to consider the twig, as I held it up before you, as a thing. But how can you answer the question of the merits of a twig as a thing? Before we can offer an evaluative judgement about a movement, or indeed say anything very much about it, we need to know from what point of view we are supposed to be considering it. We cannot consider it *neutrally*, from no particular point of view, or under some very general category, such as a thing or a phenomenon. For example, if we were asked 'Is that type of dance good?', we could not reply without knowing the kind of answer required. Is our opinion sought, for example, on whether it is good as training in physical fitness and agility, and therefore, perhaps, advantageous for athletes and other sportsmen; good therapeutically for emotionally maladjusted children; good as a 'keep fit' exercise for housewives; good for promoting social interaction; or good aesthetically?

A CONCEPTUAL, NOT AN EMPIRICAL, PROBLEM

This brings us to an important and related point, again illustrated in Spencer and White's article. They write that one reason for the paucity of empirical investigation is that dance has been regarded as an art, and therefore 'as an antithetical construct to science, not open to quantification', and later that 'Even if art were the antithesis of science, it would not mean that art was not open to empirical examination'.

It may be misleading to consider art as the antithesis of science, since, at least by implication, the negation of a thesis is still a thesis on the same logical level, or within the same category. Thus, to take an artificial example, if I were to deny your claim that a sunset can be heard, by saying that it cannot be heard, this might seem to imply that it is simply a matter of empirical fact which is being denied, i.e. that, as it happens, no one has actually heard it. Thus the denial may seem to be making a point about the limits of human auditory powers, whereas what one wants to deny is that the question makes sense, since sunsets are not the kinds of things which can be heard, any more than birdsong is the kind of thing which can be seen. Similarly, to say that some activities are empirically measurable but that artistic activities cannot be measured, while in one sense true, is at the same time highly misleading, since it may imply that there is something particularly difficult about investigating artistic activities empirically—indeed, so difficult that no one has yet succeeded, as a matter of fact, in doing so. This is the burden of Spencer and White's complaint about the lack of empirical evidence on dance. They clearly imply that the difficulty is similar to that of obtaining certain kinds of precise physical data from a distant planet. This would be an empirical difficulty, which could be solved in principle, but it so happens that science has not yet advanced far enough to overcome the technical problems involved.

But the difficulty we are considering is of a quite different kind. It consists not in the fact that science is insufficiently advanced to substantiate aesthetic judgements but in the fact that the very notion of such substantiation in this sphere is as incoherent as the notion of hearing the colours of a sunset. That is, scientific investigation is inappropriate to questions of aesthetic appreciation, hence it makes no sense to suggest that the difficulty may be overcome in due course by a more *rigorous* or ingenious application of empirical techniques. To think in this way is to have crossed the conceptual wires and thus to attempt to apply incoherent standards. This is like trying to measure the weight of heavy sarcasm or light entertainment. Jokes sometimes employ such conceptual wire-crossing, for example: 'He arrived in a furious temper and a dark green suit.'

Whereas it is true that we should demand objective substantiation for statements made about dance, it is important to recognise that not all objective substantiation is scientific. We should not confuse the fact that all human behaviour can be scientifically examined with the quite different contention that scientific examination can tell us all we want to know about human behaviour. Spencer and White again illustrate a common misapprehension on this issue, since they state that 'if something exists, it exists in quantity'. But one would be quite justified in saying that faith, hope and charity exist, and that the spirit of nationalism exists, even although in each case the question 'In what quantity?', sounds distinctly odd. The authors go even further and write of 'the quantification of concepts'. Thus even concepts, on their view, have to be measurable. Yet how does one measure the concept of space, the concept of mind, or the concept of a triangle, as opposed to this or that particular triangle? This is a clear example of the confusion which can accrue from assuming that only empirical examination can provide genuine substantiation for any kind of meaningful statement. The point was aptly captured in a cartoon of an embracing couple, with the man saying: 'I'm afraid I can't tell you how much I love you. I've left my calculator at home.'

Before leaving this part of the argument, I must make one point clear. What I wish to emphasise is that when our interest in dance concerns the justification of aesthetic judgements, then the notion of scientific examination is inappropriate. In fact, even this statement will have to be qualified shortly, but I shall ignore that complication for a moment. Nevertheless, the aesthetic is by no means the only kind of interest it is possible to have in dance. It may be, as Spencer and White suggest, that dance can be instrumental in developing, for example, physical agility and perceptual ability, and that it can have a beneficial effect on emotionally maladjusted children. Such suggestions are susceptible of scientific investigation. Nevertheless, the fact that dance is a 'piece of behaviour' does not entail the relevance of such an investigation. It depends upon the aspect of dance in which one is interested. There is a sense in which all behaviour is open to empirical investigation, but it is important to recognise that not all questions about behaviour are empirical questions.

QUANTIFICATION

The article considered above was taken as an unusually clear example of the kind of misconception about empirical substantiation which is very common and to which I want to draw attention in this chapter. We need now to consider more carefully some of the issues which have arisen, for they are of wide-ranging importance, and the source of considerable confusion in the study of human movement. In particular, it is necessary to argue for my contention that there are many aspects of human behaviour for which the notion of scientific examination is unintelligible.

A point of clarification is required here in order to avoid a serious misunderstanding. For it may be assumed that to insist that the scientific approach has its limits is to espouse the misty metaphysical conception of philosophy which it is one purpose of this book to expose as unintelligible, and harmful to the academic credentials of human-movement studies. That is, it may be assumed that my insistence that empirical investigation cannot tell us all we want to know about human behaviour, commits me to the contention that there are meaningful questions about it which are not objectively answerable to what is, at least in principle, perceivable, and therefore that the answers to such questions can be provided only in terms of the mystical or subjective. Nothing could be further from the truth. Winch (1958) puts the point this way:

> . . . it should not be assumed . . . that what I have to say must be ranked with those reactionary anti-scientific movements, aiming to put the clock back, which have appeared and flourished in certain quarters since science began. My only aim is to make sure that the clock is telling the right time, whatever it might prove to be. Philosophy . . . has no business to be anti-scientific: if it tries to be so it will succeed only in making itself look ridiculous. Such attacks are as distasteful and undignified as they are useless and unphilosophical. But equally, and for the same reasons, philosophy must be on its guard against the extra-scientific *pretensions* of science. Since science

is one of the chief shibboleths of the present age this is bound to make the philosopher unpopular; he is likely to meet a similar reaction to that met by someone who criticizes the monarchy.

It cannot be too strongly emphasised that in rejecting the mystical and subjective as unintelligible, one is not committed to the view that the only meaningful questions are scientific. I entirely endorse the scientist's exclusive preoccupation with what can be objectively substantiated or refuted. What I am concerned to point out is that there are questions which, although they are not of the kind to be examined scientifically, are still fully objective. Moreover, it is important to draw attention to the fact that failure to recognise the point may lead to seriously distorted empirical conclusions.

A good example of failure to recognise the importance of conceptual questions to empirical inquiry is to be found in *The Inequality of Man*, by Eysenck (1973), which purports to prove that there are inherent differences between black and white people with respect to intelligence. Eysenck makes it clear that, in his view, intelligence is quantifiable. Hence he has carried out a number of intelligence tests with a variety of subjects of both colours. He objects that most of those who criticise him 'tend to think in verbal terms only, and fail to criticise the model on the only grounds which are really relevant to its correctness, that is quantitative ones.' So Eysenck insists that any *legitimate* criticism be directed to the *internal* validity of his system, and he rejects as illegitimate any criticism directed at his conclusions on the *external* basis of any alleged conceptual arbitrariness. That is, he insists that, to be legitimate, any criticism of his conclusions must be able to show that there is something wrong with the empirical aspects of his work, i.e. his tests and the calculations based on them.

I shall argue that this is a good example of the point made in Chapter 1, that as a consequence of a conceptual confusion a scientist may not be measuring what he thinks he is measuring. To bring out the point clearly, let us take an artificial example. Suppose that someone were to propose that the ability to thread needles quickly is a mark of intelligence, and on this basis he conducts a series of tests as a result of which he concludes that women are more intelligent than men. You can find nothing wrong with the internal validity of his system, but you will certainly not be convinced of the validity of his conclusions as a consequence, for you will undoubtedly deny that the ability to thread needles quickly is a genuine mark of intelligence, and anyway you may point out that the tests are unfair since women are generally more practised in this activity than are men. Furthermore, you will regard it as strange if he refuses even to consider *that* as a legitimate criticism since it concerns the 'external' matter of the concept of intelligence. For instance, if he rejects your objections as irrelevant, and insists that this is how he is *defining* 'intelligence' for experimental or operational purposes, you will surely regard such a use of the term as very eccentric. Moreover, you will want to know what is the *point* of testing this ability, which bears no relation to the ordinary notion of intelligence.

Now I am not suggesting, of course, that Eysenck's misconception is as simple as that, but I do suggest that it is of the same kind. He is measuring what he calls 'Intelligence Quotient', which he equates with intelligence. Yet it is not surprising, if tendentiously misleading, that he has selected his criteria for intelligence on the basis of their relative susceptibility to scientific quantification. That is, he has chosen as criteria of intelligence, *only* those aspects which can be measured. But a consequence of such a restricted selection of criteria is that Eysenck's IQ is by no means necessarily what many of us would regard as equivalent to 'intelligence' in the normal sense. The point is that by ignoring conceptual questions he is entitled to claim only that Eysenck's IQ tests measure the ability to do Eysenck's IQ tests. It remains an open question whether IQ can be equated with intelligence. For example, Eysenck writes: 'Speed is an important aspect of intellectual work: surely it is not reasonable to take no notice of this variable which can so easily be measured.' He makes it clear that speed of response is a crucial underlying factor in all his tests. Yet one may seriously question whether speed does necessarily indicate intelligence. Indeed, experience leads one to be suspicious of those who are quick in academic debate, since it often reveals a failure adequately to consider the complexity of the issues. Even where one person regularly reaches the same conclusion more slowly than another, this does not necessarily reveal that he is less intelligent. It may be that he is more thorough, and thus rigorously considers every possible aspect of the issue. And that, if anything, indicates greater, not less, intelligence. Indeed, I am told that at one university 'intelligent' is regarded as a pejorative term, in that to apply the predicate to someone is to imply that his answers are too facile, and reveal a lack of sufficient time for adequate consideration of the relevant issues.

Now, this is not to deny that speed is often a mark of intelligence, for I am certainly not suggesting that Eysenck has selected a criterion such as the ability to thread needles, which is totally unrelated to our everyday notion of intelligence. On the contrary, what makes his case so plausible is that he adopts one of the normal criteria. Yet the mistake is of the same kind since he ignores those criteria which cannot be measured and, as there are *various* criteria for intelligence, it is misleading to offer conclusions as a consequence of considering only a one-sided selection of them. In short, by means of his tests, Eysenck purports to have proved the inequality in intelligence of black people.

But what do these tests measure? IQ, rather than intelligence, or, to put the point another way, Eysenck's specially defined, or one-sided, sense of 'intelligence' rather than what we normally call 'intelligence'.

Of course, it remains open to him to argue, as he does argue, that his notion of IQ does coincide with our normal usage of 'intelligence'. But this is *ipso facto* to *concede* the important point. For such an argument would have to be a *conceptual* one, i.e. it would require his arguing that the *meanings* of 'IQ' and 'intelligence' are equivalent. It certainly could not be achieved by exclusive preoccupation with the internal validity of his system.

If we now consider this conceptual issue it quickly becomes apparent that there are numerous manifestations of intelligence to which the notion of measurement would be absurdly inappropriate. The point is well made in an advertisement for the recruitment of naval officers. Under a photograph of three brawny ratings was written:

If you're thinking of becoming a naval officer, our ratings would like you to bear a few things in mind. They'd like you to be intelligent. And that's not just a matter of I.Q. Their lives are in your hands. It means you've got to be able to face any situation practically and sensibly—and since there can never be precedents and guidelines for every situation that can arise at sea, that means that you've always got to know precisely what you're doing.

There are many other ways in which intelligence can be revealed, but to which the suggestion of quantification would be senseless. For instance, one important mark of intelligence is the ability to understand people, but no sense could be given to the notion of quantifying such an ability.

Indeed, there is an irony in the fact that, for the reasons adduced, it might also be a mark of intelligence to refuse to take intelligence tests.

REASONS AND CAUSES

In order to understand more fully the notion of objective aspects of behaviour to which empirical investigation is inapplicable, it is necessary to recognise the distinction between explanations in terms of reasons and explanations in terms of causes. This is a complex and contentious issue so it will be impossible here to pursue it in the depth it merits. Nevertheless, it is necessary to offer an outline of it as it is central to the study of human movement, mainly because without it no adequate account can be given of intentional action.

There is a common tendency, especially for those of scientific inclination, to overlook or misconstrue the distinction between reasons and causes. Because scientific explanation is, or at least is generally assumed to be, wholly or predominantly causal, it is tempting to believe this to be the only genuine sort of explanation. However, on reflection it is immediately apparent that there is a different kind of explanation. For example, consider the case of Mrs Smith who angrily asks her husband why he has come home drunk on the evening of their wedding anniversary. She is not likely to be pacified, because she will think he has deliberately misconstrued the question, if Mr Smith replies, 'Because I drank ten pints of beer on the way home'. She is well-enough aware that the *cause* of his inebriation is his consuming a large quantity of alcohol. What she wants to know is the *reason* for it.

To take another example, a comprehensive list of the causal, physical properties of a painting is clearly irrelevant to any reason one might offer as to its artistic quality or even its subject matter. To give reasons for a critical judgement is quite different from explaining the causal properties of the paint and canvas. Similarly, since dance depends upon causal interaction between bones, muscles and joints, an exercise physiologist may be able to suggest ways in which a dancer could improve his technique. But such causal factors would be quite irrelevant to the reasons adduced for an aesthetic judgement of his dance performance. In short, although there are causally necessary conditions for artistic expression, that is certainly not to say that they are sufficient, or that artistic quality is constituted by such causal factors. To give an account of artistic meaning or of an aesthetic judgement obviously requires a quite different kind of explanation.

Again, when a player has moved a piece in a game of chess, the question, 'Why did he do that?' would not normally be understood as a request for a causal explanation, in the sense of an account in physiological, biomechanical or other such scientific terms. The questioner clearly wants to be given a reason for the move, and that is obviously not the same as a cause, in this sense.

However, although no one, presumably, would deny the distinction drawn in this very simple way, the *character* of the difference between the two possible kinds of explanation of human action is often mis-construed. It is thought that reasons are still a species of causal explanation, although of a more complicated kind than those to which reference has just been made. The explanations mentioned above refer to antecedent causes, whereas the theory we are now considering supposes that the reasons for an action can be accounted for in terms of the causal reactions to it. Thus, on this view, the question, asked of the chess player, 'Why did he do that?', where this is a request for a *reason* for, or the *meaning* of, the action, is to be answered in terms of the reactions which he anticipated as a consequence of his action. For example, psychologists commonly give this sort of account of aesthetic meaning and appreciation, in that they explain the reasons given for aesthetic judgements as consisting in people's causal reactions to works of art.

But questions of meaning, and the reasons given to explain meaning, whether of verbal terms, art or actions, cannot be reduced even to complex causes. For example, the causal effects or associations of a word are quite different from its meaning. The word 'dentist' may carry various unpleasant associations as a result of which it may cause a sinking feeling in the pit of the stomach, but that is certainly not to say that 'dentist' means 'sinking feeling in the pit of the stomach'. Wittgenstein (1953) illustrates the point in this way:

> When I say that the orders 'Bring me sugar' and 'Bring me milk' make sense, but not the combination 'Milk me sugar', that does not mean that the utterance of this combination of words has no effect. And if its effect is that the other person stares at me and gapes, I don't on that account call it the order to stare and gape, even if that was precisely the effect that I wanted to produce.

Similarly, the causal effects of a move in chess cannot constitute the reason for it. For example, a player may move a piece without being able to give a reason why he did so, yet there may still be a causal reaction. Indeed, the more bizarre his move the more likely it is to produce an effect on those watching, yet the less likely it is to make sense in terms of the game. It may have been a thoughtless aberration for which neither he nor anyone else can offer a reason. Thus the sense of a reasoned explanation certainly cannot be equated with whatever causal reaction the utterance of it may produce. Hence clearly neither kind of explanation can be reduced to the other, and only confusion can accrue from assuming that human action can be explained only in causal terms.

A more adequate account of the character of reasons will emerge from a consideration of the distinction between physical movements and intentional action, but we can begin the account here. In contrast to any explanation by reasons, in a causal account a cause and its effect are separately identifiable and do not require comprehension of the context of occurrence. Thus, for instance, the reason given for a chess move derives its sense from the context of the positions of the other pieces on the board, and from the rules and conventions of the game. That is, it requires the ascription of an intention, and that is possible only *internally*, i.e. in terms of the conventions of the game. The point can be brought out clearly by imagining what it would be like to attempt to explain the player's intention in moving the piece to someone with no comprehension of chess or any similar game. Yet the causes and causal effects of the movement of the piece could be understood even by someone with no knowledge whatsoever of this or any relevantly similar game. That is, a causal account would be *external*, in that it would not require reference to the conventions of the game. Thus it is clear that if the only explanation were a causal one, in terms of externally and independently identifiable cause and effect, it could not capture the notion of chess as a game, at least as we know it. It could not, for example, account for the ability to consider the probable consequences, in relation to the current positions of the pieces, of carrying out this move instead of another.

However, to insist on this important distinction is certainly not to deny the possibility of causal explanations. Obviously the causes and causal effects of the movement of a chess piece could be explained, for instance, in terms of nerve impulses, muscle contractions, and perhaps of psychology. It is the fact that such causal accounts could, at least in principle, be given of every action which tends to misconception, for it is tempting to assume that therefore there is no other legitimate kind of explanation of behaviour. As we have seen, this is the kind of error made by Spencer and White (1972), who insist that 'dance is a form of behaviour and, as such, is open to empirical examination'. Again: 'Even if art were the antithesis of science, it would not mean that art was not open to empirical examination . . . Dance can also be examined empirically.' This conclusion is perfectly valid, for dance movements undoubtedly can be subjected to empirical examination of the causal factors involved. But Spencer and White misconstrue the point by assuming that this is the only objective kind of explanation possible. Yet such explanations are irrelevant to questions of aesthetic appreciation of a dance performance.

Thus I certainly do not wish to be understood as denying that there may be questions which legitimately fall within the province of the psychology of aesthetics, in that there may be empirically verifiable causal effects of works of art. What I do deny is that this kind of explanation is the normal concern of those interested in the arts. Reasons for aesthetic appreciation give grounds for a response which could not intelligibly be characterised independently of the work of art. This is quite different from an account of the causal effect, which could be identified independently. To put the point another way, if aesthetic appreciation were a matter of causal reactions, then, since cause and effect are logically distinct, it would have to make sense to suppose that the *same* response could in principle be achieved by a pill, instead of the work of art. In contrast to artistic appreciation, the causal effects of a work could be specified independently of it, in that they could be ascertained and understood by someone with no comprehension whatsoever of its meaning.

To revert to a simpler example, there may be causal reactions to chess moves, but they are not normally of any interest to players or spectators. Indeed, if their interests were exclusively causal they could not be said to be interested in the *game* at all.

MOVEMENT AND ACTION

In order to understand the relevance of the foregoing discussion to the distinction between physical movement and intentional action, it may be useful to consider a related and equally plausible misconception which is revealed in the following argument.

To discover more about what physical objects are really like it is necessary to examine them as closely as possible, since it has been repeatedly revealed that the physical or chemical constitution of objects is not what it appears to be. For example, when a substance is examined under a microscope it often does not appear to be the same colour as when seen by the naked eye. White cotton, for instance, no longer looks white under a microscope, hence it is obviously a mistake to suppose that it really is white. Similarly, blood, to the naked eye, looks red, but through a microscope the separate corpuscles can be seen, which look faintly yellow. Perhaps if it were possible to go on examining cotton and blood through increasingly powerful microscopes, the colours would appear to be different again and again. Thus in fact microscopic examination reveals that objects do not really have colours at all, since the more closely they are examined the more it is discovered that their colours change.

This argument may sound convincing but it fails for reasons similar to those adduced against Eddington in Chapter 2. Different kinds of explanation are being confused here, or rather, one kind of explanation is taken to be the only kind. Normally, when we predicate colours of objects, we are not concerned with the way they might look under a microscope. However, there is a different point which I wish to bring out by the use of this example. There is a strong preconception that only *close* examination of the constitution of anything can provide the real or ultimate truth about it. Yet the premise that the best way to see the properties of an object is to scrutinise it as closely as possible is by no means self-evident. For instance, in order to discover the shape of a mountain one needs to be at a distance from it, hence it may be necessary to look at it from the opposite side of the valley.

Similarly, most of what we may want to know about a person's intentional *action* can be understood not by a narrow concentration upon his physical movement, nor by close scientific scrutiny, but by, as it were, standing back from it and seeing it in its context. And this is to make an important point about the concept of intentional action. An action, as opposed to a physical movement, can be understood only in terms of a *context*, although it may be implicit. Thus one has to 'spread the net', as one might say, to take into account the surrounding circumstances. Moreover, to explain an action, in this sense, is to explain the relationship of those contextual factors, and this can be done only by reasons, not by causes. That is, it is unintelligible to regard the context as *external* to the action, since, apart from that context it could not *be* the action it is. We have already seen an example of this in the case of the player's action of moving a piece in a game of chess. The context of the other pieces in that particular game, and especially of the conventions and rules of chess, are not *external* to the player's action, since nothing could possibly *count* as performing such an action apart from those contextual considerations. In isolation from the conventions and rules his action could be characterised only, for example, as moving one of several pieces of wood on a patterned board. But a player who performed a brilliant check-mate move would certainly deny that as an appropriate description of what he had done.

Precisely the same physical movement may count as an indefinite number of actions, according to different contexts. For example, the physical movement involved in signing my name could be various intentional actions. It could be a generous donation, or buying a car, if I were signing a cheque; it could be making a protest, if I were signing a petition; it could be an agreement to accept employment, if I were signing a contract; it could be construed as either murder or just retribution, if I were signing a death-warrant—and there is an indefinite number of other possibilities. In none of these cases could a scientific explanation tell us what the *action* is, although it could give us a causal account of the movement. There is only one movement, but it could count as many possible actions. And it is necessary, implicitly, to take into account wider considerations than the physical movement in each case in order to characterise the action. For example, without the institution of banking, and the general practices of financial exchange, whatever physical movement one were to perform, it could not count as making a donation or buying something by signing a cheque. Similarly, one needs the context of the practices involved in drawing up petitions, contracts of employment, and executions, in order for the performance of the movement to amount to the respective actions.

Our consideration of this issue can be seen to solve a problem which puzzles some physical educationists and which is a source of the tendency to slide into mystical or subjective metaphysics. For example, the question is asked: 'What makes a movement a *dance* movement, when an identical physical movement is frequently performed in gymnastics?' To assume that the difference can be discovered only by a *close* examination of the movement in the two different contexts inevitably leads to puzzlement. For there is no physical difference to be discovered. It is then natural to assume that the difference must reside in something lying *behind* the movement, which is not available to the normal senses. The usual supposition is that the difference is constituted by the 'inner feeling' of the dancer, which is absent from the identical physical movement performed by the gymnast. From that beginning there is an inexorable slide into unintelligibility. For since the inner feeling is not available to the normal senses, the only way of solving the problem of how it can be known is by resort to the archetypally metaphysical sense of intuition. But that is to have slid into incoherence, for where intuition is regarded as the only or ultimate ground of knowledge, then when one person intuits one thing and another person another, they are in a position of incommunicable subjectivism. And since this would apply to everyone else, absolutely any or no meaning or character could be attributed to movements. For it is important to be clear that the notion of intuition makes sense only by reference to what can be *observed* to happen, i.e. to the possibility of *objective* corroboration. This is not to deny that intuition can be valuable and reliable. It is to point out that such reliability depends upon whether, in general, the intuition proves to be *correct*. And that depends upon whether what is intuited accords with what can be observed to occur. Thus the intuition *itself* cannot coherently be regarded as the ultimate ground of knowledge in any sphere. The point can be illustrated by analogy with a fortune-teller, whose predictions cannot intelligibly be regarded as successful solely by virtue of the predictions *themselves*, but only by virtue of their correspondence with what objectively happens.

Yet, to repeat the point since it is so often misunderstood, this is not in the least to denigrate the value and importance of intuition. On the contrary, philosophical inquiry, scientific discovery, and perhaps every form of knowledge depends upon it, in the sense that it is only by means of such an intuitive leap that one can have any idea of the direction the argument or experimentation should take. We shall consider this issue in relation to scientific investigation later in the chapter.

It can be seen, then, why I refer to the resort to intuition as an *archetypally* metaphysical move—in the sense that it is not genuinely explanatory. When a philosopher makes appeal to intuition to solve his epistemological problems, that *ipso facto* provides good grounds for the suspicion that something has gone badly wrong with the foundation of his argument. For, as we see, at the level of philosophical explanation, the notion of intuition does no work. It merely postpones, rather than explains, the fundamental problem. This is why Wittgenstein (1953) referred to it as an 'unnecessary shuffle', since 'If intuition is an inner voice how do I know *how* I am to obey it? And how do I know that it doesn't mislead me? For if it can guide me right, it can also guide me wrong.'

With respect to our initial problem of what constitutes the specific character of a dance movement, the source of this degeneration into incoherent subjectivism is the assumption that the truth about an action is given by a close scrutiny of it. In fact what is required is not to consider it in isolation, nor to try to locate what lies behind it, but to consider what lies around it. For it is the context which gives the character of the action. It is, I think, a failure to recognise this point which contributes to a seminal misconception often encountered in discussion of the phenomenology of movement. An example will be considered in Chapter 6.

In order to remain clear about the distinction, it may be helpful to remember that an intentional action, unlike a physical movement, carries or can carry moral implications. That is, an action involves the notion of moral responsibility. For instance, a physical movement of my thumb is outside the province of moral responsibility. From that point of view it is like the movement of a branch waving on a tree, to which causal explanations are certainly relevant, but for which the notion of moral responsibility is equally unintelligible. But the intentional *action* of turning a thumb down may have been responsible for the death of a gladiator in Roman times. Again, to characterise this sort of action it is necessary to take into account the context, for nothing could possibly amount to performing such an action, even if one were to perform precisely the same physical movement of the thumb, if there were no institution of gladiatorial combat with its attendant conventions.

Indeed, to refrain from moving at all may still count as an action of various kinds, for which in certain circumstances one could be held morally responsible, for instance if one were to do nothing to help a drowning person.

As a further illustration of the point, consider the following example. Let us suppose that someone's foot comes into violent contact with my skin, and a causal explanation is provided. Such an explanation, however comprehensive, is not the same as an account of his action, for which an interpretation of the movement is required which will both determine and be determined by the attribution to him of intentions. He may have intended to kick a ball, and I inadvertently got in the way. It would carry inaccurate and misleading implications to describe this action as 'He kicked me'. On the other hand, he may have performed the movement with the intention of hurting me. So there are two possibilities for each of which the causal, scientific explanation is the same, but only one of which could be unambiguously characterised as 'He kicked me'. It is important to notice that no sense could be given to a demand for what *really* happened apart from some description of the event, which could be given only reference to the circumstances in which the movement occurred. Such a description will inevitably carry implications with respect to the question of moral responsibility, if only to absolve the agent from moral responsibility. This is quite unlike causal explanations of the movement, to which the notion of responsibility is totally inappropriate. In contradistinction, it may be difficult to formulate an account of the *action* which excludes some implication of moral responsibility.

A concentration on the physical event taken in isolation, then, is insufficient to determine the action, for which wider factors have to be considered, such as the context of its occurrence and knowledge of the agent. In order to justify an account of an intentional action one adduces reasons which consist, for instance, in showing the relationship of some of the features of the circumstances in which the incident occurred to the description one has given. In the same way, to justify an aesthetic judgement of a painting one indicates features of the painting itself which lend support to that interpretation of it. In the analogous case of chess, one gives reasons for the player's action in moving a piece by reference to the positions of the other pieces on the board, and perhaps by reference to the conventions and practice of chess playing. To return to the question of what makes a movement a dance movement, it can now be seen that the solution to the problem is given by the context of its occurrence. This movement takes place as part of a dance, in a studio, unlike that precisely similar physical movement which occurs as part of a gymnastics sequence in a gymnasium. It is the context which determines the difference between the two intentional actions. And where a movement is performed in isolation yet is still clearly recognisable as a dance movement, its character is given by the normal context of its occurrence. That is, it is recognised implicitly as the sort of movement which normally occurs in dance. This possibility of extension also justifies the description of some gymnasts as dancers, and some dancers as gymnasts. The descriptions derive from the normal context of the respective styles of movements, even although they are now performed in a different context.

We are now in a position to understand that an important characteristic of a reason consists in indicating the meaning of an action or object, i.e. what it *is*, rather than what caused it.

At the risk of repetition, let me give one more example to ensure that I have not been misunderstood. After listening to some of my arguments on the issue of this section, a scientist colleague, in the belief that he was conceding my point, amended a lecture which he gave regularly by saying 'only 5 per cent of human action is capable of scientific examination'. Quite apart from the problem of how it could be possible justifiably to arrive at such a percentage, I hope it is clear that this reveals a complete failure to grasp the point of the argument. For where 'action' is used, as in this case, to apply indiscriminately to both physical movement and intentional action, I am not saying that only *some* human action is capable of scientific examination. On the contrary, I insist that *all* human action is in principle scientifically examinable. My point is that not all questions about human action are scientific questions. To put the same point another way, of any human action it is possible in principle to provide explanations in terms both of causes and of reasons, and only the former kind of explanation falls within the province of science.

WHAT IS A FACT?

In the introduction to this chapter I said that, contrary to what is commonly supposed, scientific verification, so far from being more objective or reliable than conceptual or theoretical issues actually *depends* upon them. Although not directly relevant specifically to human movement, this section is inserted in support of that contention, and because those concerned with the sciences appear so often to be unaware of the dependence of their discipline on metaphysics, in the sense adumbrated in Chapter 1. (I draw here, to some extent, on arguments used in another book, 1974.) Scientists tend sometimes, rather condescendingly, to give the impression that they are dealing with indisputable *facts*, in contrast to those in other disciplines, especially the arts, who, they feel, indulge in mere vague speculation, and are therefore doomed to perpetual argument, with no possibility of final and decisive resolution. Indeed, the very suggestion that all science inevitably depends upon metaphysics would probably be received by most people with derision, since it is commonly assumed that scientific discovery is far superior in decisive objectivity to such speculative uncertainty. Yet the greatest problem for a scientist is often not so much to conduct experiments and make obser-vations as to interpet the results of his empirical research. This may consist of considering the extent to which these results support or detract from the explanatory value of one theory rather than another, and this may require him to take account of far more than the data which immediately confront him. Sometimes his results may suggest the formulation of a new theory which will redescribe what were previously regarded as disparate though established conclusions in such a way as to reveal important and illuminating possibilities of colligating them. A physicist, for example, may propose a higher-level theory which subsumes several lower-level ones under a richer and more comprehensive explanatory system. Nevertheless, the reasons proffered in favour of one such theory in preference to another may not necessarily be decisive, even if they are sound. So that disagreements as to the merits of rival hypotheses may be impossible to resolve solely on the basis of the results of scientific investigation.

Indeed, there is an important sense in which theoretical interpretation is a necessary precondition of any scientific fact or conclusion. Science does not consist in the collection of random data about the world by means of some sort of 'ideally' objective observation, as is popularly believed. This pervasive misconception, and the insuperable problem implicit in it, is clearly revealed by Mill (1843): 'The universe, so far as known to us, is so constituted that whatever is true in any one case, is true in all cases of a certain description; the only difficulty is, *to find what description*' (my italics).

That is, as the description, or underlying theoretical interpretation changes, so will the character of the scientific facts, since it is the underlying theoretical structure which determines what *counts* as a fact. Moreover, since there is an indefinite possibility of theoretical change, the popular notion that science produces absolute fact, or knowledge which is absolutely certain, in the sense that it could never be seriously disputed, is revealed as a myth. Hermann Bondi, Professor of Applied Mathematics, and a distinguished theoretical astronomer, puts the point in this way (1972):

> I regard the very use of the word 'fact' as misleading, because 'fact' is an emotive word which suggests something hard and firm. What we have in science is always a jumble of observation, understanding of the equipment with which the observation was carried out, interpretation and analysis. We can never clear one from another. Certain experiments that were interpreted in a particular way in their day we now interpret quite differently—but they might well have been claimed as 'facts' in those days . . . It's important to realise that in science it isn't a question of who is right and who is wrong: it is much more a question of who is useful, who is stimulating, who has helped things forward. Even after very many tests a theory remains provisional. For example, Newton's theory of gravitation was not only regarded as right: it was considered unthinkable that it could be otherwise. It was only at the very end of the 19th century, with yet more refined observation and analysis, that people began to suspect the theory ever so slightly. Now we know that it is no longer a tenable theory.

Popper, the great philosopher of science, has shown that although scientific laws can never be conclusively proven, they can be falsified, and indeed unless it *were* falsifiable a theory or law could not be genuinely scientific. Thus, to take a somewhat artificial example, 'All swans are white' could never be established as irrefutably true no matter how many confirmatory observations were recorded, but it could be refuted by the observation of just one black swan. This reveals that it is a caricature of scientific methodology to regard the scientist as conducting random, undirected experiments until the truth manifests itself. On the contrary, his discoveries logically depend upon a hypothetical, imaginative theoretical projection which he then attempts provisionally to confirm or to falsify by experiment and observation. It was a recognition of this point which induced Einstein to remark that in science imagination is more important than knowledge. In our artificial example, the hypothesis is that all swans are white. The scientist sets out with such a theoretical projection, and it is the hypothesis which *directs* the observation and experiment; it defines both their character and scope, and also the interpretation of the results. That is, it is the hypothesis which determines which kinds of experiments should be conducted, and how they should be conducted. Consequently, the logical character of scientific discovery is the converse of what is commonly supposed. For it is not so much the experimental conclusions which determine our theoretical picture of the world as that the theoretical picture determines the character of the experimental conclusions.

HUMAN MOVEMENT, KINETICS, ACTION OR BEHAVIOUR?

The main theme of this chapter reveals a problem about terminology. Strictly, in order to avoid any possible confusion, one should, perhaps, conceive of two quite distinct strata, with 'movement' exclusively in the stratum 'causal', 'empirical', 'scientific'; and 'action' exclusively in the stratum 'reason', 'intention', 'conceptual'. However, it seemed to me that it would offend too much against general usage to deny that there can be causal explanations of actions, and too much against common usage in the field of human movement to deny that movements can be intentional. So, in general, I use the terms indiscriminately, and indicate the distinction required by prefacing them with 'physical', in the case of 'movement', and 'intentional' or 'voluntary' in the case of 'action', only when an issue of importance hangs on it, and when what I intend is not clear from the context. Sometimes, in order to avoid confusion, I use 'behaviour' to operate neutrally, as it were, between the two concepts.

The crucial relevance of the conceptual in the study of human movement carries important implications for the curriculum. Where there has been academic study in this comparatively new field it has traditionally been predominantly or even exclusively of a scientific nature. This tendency persists, at least in Britain, North America and Australasia. It will be clear from what has been said earlier in the chapter that I certainly do not wish to denigrate the importance of the scientific study of human movement. Nevertheless, I hope that enough has been said to reveal that an *exclusive* concentration on the scientific examination of human movement at best is one-sided, since it ignores a whole range of equally important, and equally objective aspects, and at worst it is conducive to the kinds of gravely damaging misconception of which we have exposed some examples in this chapter. It is to be hoped that, as a matter of some urgency, philosophy will be included as central to the study of human movement, and that it will form a compulsory part of every first-degree course in this field.

A related problem concerns nomenclature. Departments and faculties are most commonly entitled 'Human Movement' or 'Human Kinetics'. It will be clear from the argument of this chapter that such terms already carry implications of a scientific or causal interest in the subject. It might seem preferable, in order to include the inevitable conceptual issues which arise, to create the title 'Human Action Studies'. Yet in that case we should have the opposite problem, for this would imply the exclusion of empirical, causal inquiry, and a concern solely for conceptual issues. 'Human Behaviour Studies' has been suggested as a term which could operate across the boundaries, but even this carries empirical connotations as, for example, in behaviourism. I know of no title which would indicate an equal concern for both empirical and conceptual issues. However, this need pose no great problem as long as we are clear that no programme of study will be adequate which does not include both modes of inquiry. In general, in this book and elsewhere, I use the term 'human movement', and this need create no confusion as long as it is clearly understood that conceptual considerations are ineliminable. Moreover, since this and 'Human Kinetics' now appear to be increasingly the most popular titles for departments and faculties, it is probably wise to try to standardise. Nevertheless, in view of the predominant over-emphasis on the sciences, it is of the first importance to stress the need for the inclusion of courses in the conceptual issues which arise in the study of human movement, and to urge the leading academics in this field to take positive steps to encourage a wide range of conceptual inquiry. Moreover, where teaching and research in philosophy are included, they should be undertaken only by those with a rigorous training in the discipline. As I indicated in Chapter 1, there is a good deal of pretentious verbosity which passes for the 'philosophy' of sport, physical education and dance, and which has to be eradicated before a constructive, genuinely philosophical enterprise can realise the potential of the discipline in this field of study.

REFERENCES: CHAPTER 5

Best, D., *Expression in Movement and the Arts* (London: Lepus Books, Henry Kimpton Publishers, 1974).

Bondi, H., 'The achievement of Sir Karl Popper', *The Listener*, vol. 88, no. 2265 (24 August 1972).

Eysenck, H. J., *The Inequality of Man* (London: Temple Smith, 1973).

Mill, J. S., *System of Logic* (London: 1843).

Spencer, L. and White, W., 'Empirical examination of dance in educational institutions', *British Journal of Physical Education*, vol. 3, no. 1 (January 1972).

Winch, P., *The Idea of a Social Science and Its relation to Philosophy* (London: Routledge & Kegan Paul, 1958).

Wittgenstein, L., *Philosophical Investigations* (Oxford: Basil Blackwell, 1953).

Chapter 6

The Essence of Movement

The importance of recognising the limitations of empirical investigation resides not only in revealing the conceptual confusions of some scientific inquiry but also in exposing plausible misconceptions of an opposite extreme which are often encountered among non-scientists. Some phenomenologists misconstrue their recognition of those limitations by denying that empirical methodology can explain anything that really matters about human movement. They assume that only a close concentration on the movement itself will reveal its essential character, and that empirical examination is inevitably restricted to relatively superficial external aspects of it. The assumption that there must be such an underlying essence can lead to damaging misconceptions about the nature of human movement and its study. Such an assumption stems partly from a failure to provide an adequate account of those aspects of behaviour to which empirical investigation is inappropriate. As we saw in Chapter 5, there is a danger of misconception in the assumption that the truth is always to be found by digging *deeply*. Wittgenstein (1953) expresses the point in this way:

> The aspects of things that are most important for us are hidden because of their simplicity and familiarity. One is unable to notice something—because it is always before one's eyes. We fail to be struck by what, once seen, is most striking and most powerful.

THE DEFINITIONAL FALLACY

A common fallacy which is sometimes related to that adumbrated above is the general demand for definitions, i.e. the tendency to assume that one may be said to understand the meaning of a word only if one can define it verbally. Although I have considered this issue in another book (1974) it is worth repeating the main outlines here since the misconception is so prevalent. The assumption is, then, that to know the meaning of any general term is to be able to state those conditions which are separately necessary and together sufficient for all correct instances of its use.

It is important, first, to be clear about precisely what is required of a definition. It can be said that 'D' is a definition of 'A' only if the two terms are logically equivalent, by which I mean that all cases of 'A' are necessarily cases of 'D', and conversely, or, to put the point another way, that in all contexts 'D' can be substituted for 'A', and 'A' for 'D', without change of meaning. Now I do not wish to deny that precise definitions can be given of some terms. For example, a bachelor can be defined as an unmarried man, and a triangle can be defined as a plane figure bounded by three straight sides. What I do deny is that definitions can be given of all or even the great majority of terms, despite the common assumption that, in general, one cannot be said to have a clear understanding of the meaning of a term unless one can define it. As we saw in Chapter 1, it is important to be clear about the meanings of the terms we employ, but it is equally important to recognise that being clear about meaning is by no means the same as being able to produce a verbal definition. There is a great deal that could be said on this topic, but I shall restrict myself to three arguments, each of which is sufficient to show that the general demand for definitions is misconceived.

(1) We are in practice unable to produce definitions of most of the words we use, although we are well aware of their meanings. For example, we are unable to define verbally the names of the primary colours, but this does not prevent our knowing what 'red' means and using it correctly. Moreover, it is significant that we certainly learned, as children, the meanings of most words without being provided with definitions.

(2) The person who says he must search for a definition before he can legitimately be said to know the meaning of a term, in practice inevitably contradicts himself. He puts the cart before the horse, since the ability to recognise that a definition is correct, or to raise counter-examples and objections to it, presupposes that he must know the meaning of the term *before* he finds the definition, even if he should succeed.

(3) Even the simple case of the triangle which we have considered depends upon an understanding of the *non*-defined meanings of the words used in the definition—words such as 'plane', 'bounded', 'straight', and so on. In short, if a definition had to be provided before we could understand the meaning of *every* word then we should never be able to understand the meaning of *any* word. Every word in the definition would have to be defined in words, each of which would have to be defined in words, each of which would have to be defined in words, each of which . . . and so on to infinity. This is another example of a vicious infinite regress, which was explained in Chapter 4. As we saw then, an argument which can be shown to depend upon such a regress has *ipso facto* been shown to be invalid, since it can

never even begin. So the ability to give a definition presupposes that the words which comprise it are understood *without* definition.

This should be sufficient to explode the surprisingly pervasive and tenacious myth that it should be possible in general to provide definitions of the terms we use. An example is provided by Lange (1970) who, in an article entitled 'The nature of dance', considers some of the better-known definitions of dance, and remarks that it is striking how much they vary. Yet this variety reveals not so much the difficulty of defining *dance* specifically as the more fundamental misconception concerning definitions. In short, the problem is created not by the nature of dance but by the common confusion of meaning with definition.

It is to be hoped, then, that enough has been said at least to induce considerable caution about the demand for definitions. It is a common experience, in discussion, to be asked to define one's terms, yet it is ironic that those who ask are usually unclear about what is required of a definition. So it may be a good ploy to ask the questioner to define 'definition'. Such a definition is provided above, but since he has asked such a question it is unlikely that he will be aware of it.

Nevertheless, it should not be thought that the search for definitions is always pointless. In some cases it may be possible to find one, and even where it is not, the attempt to find one may bring out salient features of the concept in question. The danger of misconception arises from the unquestioned assumption that there *must* be such a definition to be found.

THE MOVEMENT ITSELF

The article by Spencer and White (1972), discussed in Chapter 5, reveals a clear general position not only about the study of human movement but about the substantiation of any assertion. The authors make two major points: (1) They complain that there are many unsupported claims made for dance; (2) They insist that such claims, like any other statement, in order to be meaningful should be substantiated by empirical examination and quantification. For instance, they write: 'The position taken in this paper is that dance is a form of behaviour, and, as such, is open to empirical examination. That is, if something exists, it exists in quantity.'

In order to understand the source of the misconception which is our primary concern in this chapter, we need to remind ourselves of the plausibility of the case proposed by Spencer and White. It could be argued as follows: 'Dance is a form of behaviour. All forms of behaviour can be scientifically examined. Therefore dance can be scientifically examined.' This argument is undeniably valid, yet, as we saw in Chapter 5, although all behaviour can be scientifically examined that is certainly not to say that the only legitimate explanations of behaviour are scientific. Spencer and White fail to recognise this point and clearly do regard this as the only way in which statements made about human behaviour may be genuinely verified, since no aspect of it which is not open to empirical quantification can, in their view, be said even to exist.

Yet, in order to reject this sort of conclusion, some writers feel constrained to adopt an equally misconceived attitude, which in fact turns out to be the opposite side of precisely the same coin, in that they inadvertently share with their opponents the most damaging underlying assumption. A classic example occurs in an article by Harper (1973), significantly entitled 'Movement and measurement: the case of the incompatible marriage'. Harper is well aware that there is something particularly important about human movement to which the notion of empirical examination is inappropriate, yet he seriously misconceives the point: 'Implicit in nearly all of the human movement literature is the following presupposition: Human movement is accessible in sense experience, i.e. the movement of one person can be perceived by another.'

He goes on to state that this presupposition is patently false because it fails to take account of the important distinction between the possibility of sensing *things* which move or are moved, and the impossibility of sensing the *movements* of them. He agrees that we can see horses running, birds flying, rocks falling, and human beings walking, but he insists that we cannot see the movements themselves: '... what one actually comes upon in sense experience are various objects in the world, including human beings, which are moving or are moved, *and not the movements of them*.'

This part of his argument is so immediately implausible that one already suspects that it is a consequence of a more significant, underlying misconception concerning sense-perception and objectivity. For, clearly, to speak of the movement of John is just another way of speaking of John's moving. However, Harper produces a more plausible argument by reference to the distinction between what is experienced, and the experiencing of it. He writes:

> Regardless of how the researcher reasons, however, if he takes up the empirical methodology, he is caught in a flat contradiction. It is essential to empirical techniques that knowledge is to be ultimately grounded in sense experience. If the human movement researcher is willing to assume movement to be available in sense experience, then adoption of empirical techniques may be appropriate to the object. But, as we have pointed out, human movement is not of the

nature to be sensed by another. And thus the researcher appears to be caught choosing a method which relies upon what is studied to be sense given, but turning it towards an object which is not sensible. Under these imperfect conditions the nature of human movement could not ever be known.

This quotation clearly reveals that Harper assumes there is an essential nature which underlies human movement yet which, since it cannot be perceived, is beyond the scope of empirical methodology. This leads him to conclude that in this sphere such methodology can yield *no* positive knowledge and is therefore irrelevant to the study of human movement since it can only presuppose its essential nature:

With regard to ... the movement [experienced], empirical research must fail to yield positive results as the *essential natures* of the various movements under examination are presupposed in order for empirical procedures to even be employed. In order even to find individual instances of an activity, one must already have presupposed an *essential knowledge* of the activity to be analyzed. Otherwise how could one know he is studying leaping and not running, tennis and not golf, wrestling and not eating? One knows what each of these activities are or he could never find reliable instances of them. And thus, the empiricist is caught presupposing the *essential nature* of what he is analyzing and thereby cannot inspect or clarify that *essential nature*. The *essential differences* between activities remain unnoticed and therefore unexamined. (my italics)

Spencer and White insist that any statement made about human movement, to make sense at all, must be open to empirical examination. In order to reject that kind of misconception Harper succumbs to another by insisting that, on the contrary, since empirical investigation cannot explain the essence it is altogether irrelevant to our understanding of human movement. But the assumption on which he bases the conclusion, namely that the essence of movement is not available to sense-perception, leads him to the startling conclusion that movement cannot even exist. In his own words: 'In itself, a movement cannot exist, that is, cannot be in time and space. Therefore it cannot be available to sense experience as it is not anywhere at any time.' One can, perhaps, already begin to appreciate that this is in fact the opposite side of the *same* coin as Spencer and White's, since, it will be recalled, they also insisted that 'if something exists, it exists in quantity'. But this is to anticipate the argument, and I shall return to the point.

Harper concludes that the reason for the unsatisfactory state of human-movement studies is that empirical techniques have prevented human-movement researchers from understanding clearly the essential nature of the subject matter. If he were right, those who study movement from, for example, psychological, sociological and physiological points of view are obviously wasting their time, since what they are attempting to examine cannot even be perceived.

A major source of his extraordinary conclusion is Harper's assumption that there must be an essence of movement to be found, and since it cannot be perceived he can presume only that it must lie outside the realm of sense-experience altogether. This is a clear case of the kind of misconception considered in Chapter 5, of assuming that the truth about an action or movement is to be found by concentrating *closely* upon it. Such a misapprehension is also at the heart of much phenomenological thought, which mistakenly assumes that it makes sense to suggest that it is possible to exclude contextual and therefore conceptual factors in order to concentrate on what it supposes to be the movement *itself*. Wittgenstein (1953) puts the point in this way: 'In order to find the real artichoke we divested it of its leaves.' Similarly, in order to find the essence of human movement, Harper and such phenomenologists try to divest it of all that is available to sense-perception. But instead of finding the essence we discover that there is nothing left.

Of course it is true, as we saw in the preceding chapter, that empirical methodology cannot tell us *everything* about movement. Moreover, it is true that where the scientist is concerned to examine intentional action, *what* that action is has to be presupposed, and therefore it cannot itself be explained by scientific examination. Hence to imagine that empirical methodology can comprehensively explain human action or movement is to be fundamentally mistaken. Yet that is certainly not to say that the empirical sciences cannot explain what really matters, or anything that really matters, about human movement. There are many aspects of human movement to which the notion of scientific explanation is unintelligible, but only an essentialist presupposition will lead to the conclusion that therefore the sciences have *nothing* significant to say about it. On the contrary, there are also many important aspects of human movement which *do* lie within the scope of scientific explanation.

EXPERIENCE AND OBSERVABLE CRITERIA

Although Spencer and White on the one hand, and Harper on the other, appear to be diametrically opposed, we have already had reason to suspect that in fact their extremes of opposition stem from a shared underlying presupposition. And further examination confirms that suspicion, for it can be shown that their respective positions are in fact opposite sides of the same misconceived coin. The point can be brought out in this way:

> Spencer and White: If an aspect of human movement is not open to empirical investigation then it is not answerable to sense-perception, in which case it cannot be said to exist.
>
> Harper: If an aspect of human movement is not open to empirical investigation then it is not answerable to sense-perception, in which case it cannot be said to exist. Since the essential nature of human movement is not open to empirical investigation, it must be beyond sense-perception and thus cannot be said to exist in time and space.

It is the agreed presupposition which, although commonly encountered, and central to much phenomenology, is the source of the confusion. For, as we saw in Chapter 5, there are many aspects of behaviour which are not open to empirical investigation but which are nevertheless objectively perceivable. For example, an empirical investigation could not determine the character of the intentional action performed by the physical movement involved in signing one's name. But not even the most hard-headed scientist who received by cheque a gift of £100 as a result would, presumably, want to deny its objective existence on the grounds that it could not be empirically verified.

As I conceded above, Harper's most plausible argument rests on the distinction he draws between what is experienced and the experiencing of it. He adduces this distinction in order to show that the *experiencing* cannot be objectively perceivable. This carries plausibility because it is true that no sense can be made of the suggestion that someone else could observe my *experiencing*, even if he can observe *what* I am experiencing. But this argument does not achieve what Harper wants, and indeed it can be shown to undermine his whole position. As we have seen, he clearly regards the experiencing as the essence of an action or movement, and that which determines its character. Yet even given a coherent philosophical account of experiencing, namely as identified by typical manifestation in observable behaviour, it is unintelligible to suppose that it can be this which determines the character of the action. That is, it cannot coherently be supposed that simply having an experience while performing it is what determines what an action is. In fact, the opposite is true. It is not that the experience determines the action, but that the context of occurrence determines not only the character of the action but also the character of the experience. Nothing could amount to the action, and therefore the experiencing, of a checkmate move without the context of chess. Thus, although Harper is right to point out that empirical investigation has to presuppose, and therefore cannot determine, whether an action is 'leaping and not running, tennis and not golf, wrestling and not eating', to appeal to the *experiencing* as that which explains the character of an action is equally misconceived since in fact it can explain nothing. For, in his terms, the experiencing cannot coherently be regarded as logically distinct from what is experienced.

To explain what is meant by this last remark will also allow me to expose the misconception inherent in an objection which is sometimes raised against some of my own work, such as the argument of Chapter 7, namely, that I do not distinguish between the spectator and the performer, or that I concentrate my attention too much on the spectator and do not adequately consider the experience of the performer. Such an objection is based upon deep confusions about mental concepts which we shall consider more fully in Chapters 8 and 9. However, the argument of this chapter already reveals an outline of the fundamental misconception in this way of thinking, since implicit in the objection is the notion that it makes sense to suppose that while the context may be important for the spectator, it is the experience *itself* which is important for the performer, and this is a purely subjective matter which can be understood solely by the performer in isolation from any contextual considerations. And this, of course, is why Harper assumes that the experiencing, and therefore, on his view, the character of the intentional action, cannot be answerable to sense-perception.

Yet the notion of the experience *itself*, in isolation from its normal, perceivable context is unintelligible. For again, no experience could possibly *count* as that of making a checkmate move in isolation from the context of the rules and conventions of chess. Precisely similar considerations apply to Harper's examples of experiencing the movements involved in playing tennis and golf. Apart from the relevant rules and conventions, whatever movements were performed, nothing could possibly count as having the same experiences. As Wittgenstein (1953) puts it:

> The very fact that we should so much like to say: 'This is the important thing'—while we point privately to the sensation—is enough to shew how much we are inclined to say something which *gives no information*. (my italics)

Elsewhere (1969) he writes: 'What is the proof that I *know* something? Most certainly not my saying that I know it ... An inner experience cannot show me that I know something.' On the contrary, it is the characteristic external circumstance of its occurrence which, as it were, tells *me* what experience I am having. This is not to deny that one could *have* the experience in different circumstances and outside the normal context. It is to insist that the experience could not be *identified*, and therefore that nothing could possibly count as the same '*experiencing*', without reference to the normal context of its occurrence. For example, on producing a convincing argument in a debate, someone might say: 'It felt exactly like making a checkmate move.' Although the experience now occurs in a debate, the normal context is necessary for such a characterisation of it. Moreover, even in these different circumstances it must be possible to offer in justification some link with the normal context in order for such an assertion to be intelligible.

To put the point another way, if the mover should refer to the experience by saying, while performing the movement: 'It feels like *this*', there is no way of distinguishing the 'it' from the 'this'. That is, the performer's experience is determined *for him too* by the perceivable movement in the context of its occurrence. It is for this reason that it is necessary to concentrate a philosophical examination of experience on such *observable* criteria. But to assume that this reveals a concern solely or predominantly with the spectator shows a failure to appreciate why it is necessary. I insist on the central place of personal experience, and therefore I am equally concerned with the performer. To concentrate attention on perceivable behaviour is certainly not to denigrate the 'experiencing' but, on the contrary, is the only intelligible way to provide an account of it. As we have seen, a consequence of misconstruing the importance of such observable criteria is that the experience of movement disappears altogether. (I explain more fully in another book, 1974, the crucial relation of observable criteria to personal experience.)

Harper's misconception, then, stems from two erroneous assumptions: (1) that there must be an underlying essential nature of human movement; and (2) that to be objectively answerable to sense-perception is to be open to empirical investigation. With these presuppositions he can hardly avoid the conclusion that the essential nature of movement cannot exist in space and time, for otherwise it would be available to sense-perception and thus, on his second assumption, open to empirical investigation.

It is most important to see not so much that his conclusion is mistaken as what led him to it, for it is based on plausible assumptions which are widely accepted without question in the field of human movement. I shall say a little more about the danger inherent in the former assumption in a moment. In relation to the latter, it is strange how persistent and pervasive is the misconception that 'objective' necessarily implies 'scientific', i.e. that *only* scientific explanations can be objective. I hope that enough has been said in this chapter and the last to expose that misconception, and to show how it almost inexorably leads to unintelligible subjectivism. To repeat the point, an account of an intentional action such as signing a cheque is as objective as an account of a physical movement, even although the former is not open to scientific explanation.

Each of the theses about the study of human movement which have been considered in this and the previous chapter is drawing attention, even if misguidedly, to an important aspect overlooked by the other. Thus it should not be thought that the mistakes which have been revealed are simple or stupid mistakes. On the contrary, such misconceptions are frequently encountered, and usually not so thoroughly worked out. The somewhat implausible conclusions are a consequence of taking a valid point to an invalid extreme.

To revert to the notion of an underlying essential nature of human movement, I was once involved in negotiations with a validating committee which was considering proposals for a degree in human-movement studies. At one point the suspicion was voiced that such a subject of study amounted to what was called a 'conceptually arbitrary topic'. So far as it was possible to discover what was meant by this, it appeared to reveal a vague feeling that there was no essential nature, central core, or unitary methodology here. Yet in that case the study of human movement is no more conceptually arbitrary than sociology, which inevitably incorporates the insights of disciplines such as history, geography, anthropology, psychology and philosophy in order to provide an understanding of human society and social relationships. If we were to divest the artichoke of sociology of the leaves of its contributory disciplines in order to discover its central core, or essential nature, there would be nothing left. Indeed, if the academic credentials of a subject of study depended upon its employing a unitary methodology, the only possible survivor of the exodus from universities would be pure mathematics. The sciences, for example, inevitably employ mathematics; geography involves the methodology of history, mathematics and the sciences; history involves the sciences and geography. A subject is none the less legitimately academic if it needs to call upon various contributory disciplines for enlightenment.

The article which has been the principal concern of this chapter was entitled: 'Movement and measurement: the case of the incompatible marriage' (Harper, 1973). As I have tried to show, the marriage is not in the least incompatible. On the contrary, eternal wedded bliss is assured as long as each partner clearly understands the character of the other.

What is time? St Augustine confessed that if no one asked him he knew, but when he tried to explain it, then he became puzzled. I suggest that we are in a similar case with human movement. It is what we see it is. There is no underlying essential nature, and no over-ridingly important academic methodology for its study.

What is human movement *in itself*?

Such a loaded question, as we have seen, may tend to such an excessive and misguided determination to uncover its essence that human movement will disappear altogether.

REFERENCES: CHAPTER 6

Best, D., *Expression in Movement and the Arts* (London: Lepus Books, Henry Kimpton Publishers, 1974).

Harper, W., 'Movement and measurement: the case of the incompatible marriage', *Quest* (June 1973).

Lange, R., 'The nature of dance', *Laban Guild Magazine* (May 1970).

Spencer, L. and White, W., 'Empirical examination of dance in educational institutions', *British Journal of Physical Education*, vol. 3, no. 1 (January 1972).

Wittgenstein, L., *Philosophical Investigations* (Oxford: Basil Blackwell, 1953).

Wittgenstein, L., *On Certainty* (Oxford: Basil Blackwell, 1969).

Chapter 7

The Aesthetic in Sport

INTRODUCTION

There appears to be a considerable and increasing interest in looking at various sporting activities from the aesthetic point of view. In this chapter I shall examine a central characteristic of paradigm cases of objects of the aesthetic attitude, namely works of art, in order to see to what extent it is applicable to sport. Finally, I shall consider the question of whether sports in general, or at least those sports in which the aesthetic is ineliminable, can legitimately be regarded as forms of art. It will be shown that discussion of this topic is confused by a failure to recognise the significance of the distinction between the aesthetic and the artistic.

THE AESTHETIC POINT OF VIEW

It might be asked whether all sports can be considered from the aesthetic point of view, when one takes account of the great and increasingly varied range of such activities. That question at least can be answered clearly in the affirmative, for any object or activity can be considered aesthetically—cars, mountains, even mathematical proofs and philosophical arguments.

This raises a point discussed in Chapter 5, that it is less conducive to error to regard the aesthetic as a way of perceiving an object or activity than as a constituent feature of it. I mention this because the term 'aesthetic content' is often used, and it carries the misleading implication that the aesthetic is some sort of element which can be added or subtracted. In order to clarify the point it may be worth considering a way in which the notion of aesthetic content was once defended. It was argued that the aesthetic cannot be merely a point of view since this fails to account for the fact that some objects and activities are more interesting aesthetically than others. Thus, it was said, there must be aesthetic content since, for instance, the appearance of a car could be affected by altering physical features of it, and in a similar way gracefulness could be added to or subtracted from a movement.

A factor which may well contribute to confusion on this issue is a failure to distinguish two ways in which 'aesthetic' is used. These can be broadly characterised as (1) evaluative, and (2) conceptual. An example of the former is: 'Borzov is an aesthetic athlete.' This is to use the term in a positive evaluative way, and is roughly equivalent to 'graceful', or 'aesthetically pleasing'. But it is clearly the latter usage which is our concern, and this includes both the beautiful and the ugly; the graceful and the clumsy; the aesthetically interesting and the aesthetically uninteresting. Thus whatever one's opinion of the appearance of the car, it has to be considered from the aesthetic point of view in order for any relevant judgement to be offered.

Now certainly it does not necessarily indicate a misapprehension to use the term 'aesthetic content'. It depends what is meant by it, and there are two possibilities:

(1) To assert that A is part of the content of B would normally imply that A is a constituent feature or component of B, and that therefore a close examination of B will reveal it. This naturally leads to the kind of error discussed in Chapters 5 and 6. For, since statements about aesthetic content cannot be supported by empirical investigation, there will be a strong temptation to assume either that the aesthetic content is non-physical and somehow lying behind the physical object or activity, or that the aesthetic is a purely subjective content, not in the object itself but solely in the mind of the perceiver. And since in neither case can any sense be given to the notion of justification of aesthetic judgements, this is to reduce them to vacuity.

(2) However, if the term 'aesthetic content' is used to make the point that it is only by reference to objective features that aesthetic judgements can be justified, then the notion is unexceptionable. There is a complex issue here, which involves the distinction between physical movements and actions, which was explained in Chapter 5. To make the point briefly, precisely the same physical movements may be aesthetically pleasing in one context yet displeasing in another. For example, one may regard a series of movements in a dance as poor aesthetically until it is pointed out that one has misinterpreted the performance. Under the different interpretation they can now be seen as superb. Although there is no physical difference in the movements, the revised judgement is based upon the way in which the new interpretation has determined a different context. Nevertheless, the new interpretation and aesthetic judgement depend solely upon *objective* aspects of the movements. (I consider the nature of the objective reasons given in support of aesthetic judgements in another book, 1974.)

Thus aesthetic judgements are certainly answerable in this way to observable physical features, and if the point of using the term 'aesthetic content' is to emphasise the fact no confusion need arise. However, since it is so frequently used in, or with the misleading implications of, the former sense, it is, in my view, wiser to eschew the term.

THE AESTHETIC CONCEPT

Although anything can be considered from the aesthetic aspect, some activities and objects are more centrally of aesthetic interest than others. Works of art, to take a paradigm case, are primarily of aesthetic interest, although even they can be considered from other points of view. For instance, paintings are commonly considered as an investment. Hence we need to ask what distinguishes the aesthetic from other ways of looking at objects. One important characteristic is that the aesthetic is a non-functional or non-purposive concept. To take a central example again, when we are considering a work of art from the aesthetic point of view we are not considering it in relation to some external function or purpose it serves. It cannot be evaluated aesthetically according to its degree of success in achieving some such extrinsic end. By contrast, when a painting is considered as an investment, then it is assessed in relation to an extrinsic end, namely that of maximum appreciation in financial value.

This characteristic of the aesthetic immediately raises an insuperable objection to theories which propose an oversimple relation between sport and the aesthetic by identifying them too closely. For example, it is sometimes claimed that sport just *is* an art form (for examples, see Anthony, 1968), and it has been suggested that the aesthetic is the concept which unifies all the activities subsumed under the heading of physical education (see Carlisle, 1969). But there are many sports, indeed the great majority, which are like the painting considered as an investment in that there is an aim or purpose which can be identified independently of the way it is accomplished. That is, the *manner* of achievement of the primary purpose is of little or no significance as long as it comes within the rules. For example, it is normally far more important for a football or hockey team *that* a goal is scored than *how* it is scored. In very many sports of this kind the over-riding factor is the achievement of some such independently specifiable end, since that is the mark of success.

This non-purposive character of the aesthetic is often misunderstood. Such a misunderstanding is manifested in the commonly supposed consequence that therefore there can be no point in art. The presupposition underlying this misunderstanding is that an activity can intelligibly be said to be of point or value only in relation to some external purpose towards which it is directed. Now in cases where such an extrinsic end is the primary consideration, evaluation does depend on it. As we have seen, a painting considered solely as an investment would be evaluated entirely according to its degree of success in achieving maximum capital appreciation. Where the attainment of the end is the over-riding consideration, the means of attaining it obviously becomes relatively unimportant. It would not matter, for instance, what sort of painting it was as long as the end was realised. Similarly, if someone should wish to improve the petrol consumption of his car by changing the carburetter, the design of the new one and the materials from which it is made would be unimportant as long as it succeeded in giving maximum mileage per gallon.

However, the purpose of art cannot be specified in this way, although the misapprehension we are now considering stems from the mistaken assumption that the point of an activity *must* somehow be identifiable as an end or purpose distinct from the activity itself. Yet where art, or more generally the aesthetic, is concerned, the distinction between means and end is inapplicable. For instance, the question 'What is the purpose of that novel?', can be answered comprehensively only in terms of the novel itself. It might be objected that this is not entirely true, since the purpose of some novels could be given as, for example, exposing certain deleterious social conditions. But this objection misses the point I am trying to make, for if the purpose is the external one of exposing those social conditions then in principle it could equally well, or perhaps better, be realised in other ways, such as the publication of a social survey or a political speech. The report of the social survey is evaluated solely by reference to its purpose of effectively conveying the information, whereas this would be quite inappropriate as a standard for the aesthetic evaluation of a novel. To put the same point another way, from the point of view of efficient conveying of information, the precise form and style of writing of the report is unimportant except in so far as it affects the achievement of that purpose. One report could be as good as another, although the style of writing or compilation was different from or even inferior to the other. There could not be a parallel situation in art in which, for example, one poem might be said to be as good as another although not so well written. This is an aspect of the complex problem of form and content in the arts. To put it briefly, there is a peculiarly intimate connection between the form of an object of aesthetic appreciation, i.e. the particular medium of expression, and its content, i.e. what is expressed in it. So that in art there cannot be a change of form of expression without a corresponding change in what is expressed. It is important to recognise that this is a logical point. For even if one way of writing the report were the clearest and most efficient, this is a mere contingent matter since it is always possible that a better method may be devised. But it is not a contingent matter that the best way of expressing the content of Solzhenitsyn's *One Day in the Life of Ivan Denisovich* is in the particular form of that novel, i.e. it would make no sense to suggest that its content could be more effectively conveyed in another way. So that the question becomes:

'What is the purpose of this particular way of exposing the social conditions?' The end cannot be specified as 'exposing such and such social conditions', but only as 'exposing such and such social conditions in this particular way and no other'. And to give a comprehensive account of what is meant by 'in this particular way and no other' one would have to produce nothing less than the whole novel. The end cannot be identified apart from the manner of achieving it, and that is another way of saying that the presupposition encapsulated in the question, of explanation in terms of purposive action directed onto an external end, is unintelligible in the sphere of aesthetics. In short, in an important sense the answer to 'What is the purpose of that novel?' will amount to a rejection of the question.

A further objection, which has important implications for the aesthetic in sport, might be that in that case how can we criticise a work of art if it can be justified only in terms of itself and there is nothing else with which it can be compared? There is a great deal to be said about the common misapprehension that to engage in critical reasoning is necessarily to generalise (see Bambrough, 1973). It is sufficient for my argument to recognise that critical appreciation of art consists largely in giving reasons why particular features contribute so effectively to or detract from *this particular* work of art. The important point for our purposes is to see again that the end is inseparable from the means of achieving it, for any suggested improvement is given in terms of the particular work of art in question. Another way of putting this point is to say that every feature of a work of art is relevant to the aesthetic assessment of it, whereas when we are judging something as a means to an end, there are irrelevant features of the means, or equally effective alternative means, of achieving the required end. To say that X is an irrelevant feature is always a criticism of a work of art, whereas this is not true of a functional object.

It is true that the aim in a sport cannot be considered in isolation from the rules or norms of that particular sport. Scoring a goal in hockey is not just a matter of getting the ball between the opponents' posts, but requires conformity to the laws of the game. Such requirements are implicit in the meaning of the term 'scoring a goal'. Nevertheless, in contrast to a work of art, within those limits there are many ways of achieving the end, i.e. of scoring a goal, in hockey.

THE GAP: PURPOSIVE AND AESTHETIC SPORTS

At this point we need to direct our attention to the difference between types of sporting activities with respect to the relative importance of the aesthetic. On the one hand, there are those sports, which I shall call 'purposive' and which form the great majority, where the aesthetic is normally relatively unimportant. This category would include football, climbing, track and field events, orienteering and squash. In each of these sports the purpose can be specified independently of the manner of achieving it as long as it conforms to the limits set by the rules or norms—for example, scoring a goal and climbing the Eiger. Even in such sports as these, of course, certain moves or movements, indeed whole games or performances, can be considered from the aesthetic point of view, but it is not central to the activity. It should be recognised that this is a logical point. For example, an activity could obviously still count as football even if there were never a concern for the aesthetic. By contrast, it could not count as football if no one ever tried to score a goal. That is, in these sports it is the independently specifiable purpose which at least largely defines the character of the activity, and the aesthetic is incidental.

On the other hand, there is a category of sports in which the aim cannot be specified in isolation from the aesthetic, for example, synchronised swimming, trampolining, gymnastics, figure-skating and diving. I shall call these 'aesthetic' sports since they are similar to the arts in that their purpose cannot be considered apart from the manner of achieving it. There is an intrinsic end which cannot be identified apart from the means. Consider, for example, the notion of a vault in formal gymnastics. The end is not simply to get over the box somehow or other, even if one were to do so in a clumsy way and collapse afterwards in an uncontrolled manner. The way in which the appropriate movements are performed is not incidental but central to such a sport. That is, the aim cannot be specified simply as 'getting over the box', but only in terms of the manner of achievement required. Indeed, aesthetic norms are implicit in the meaning of terms like 'vault' and 'dive', in that to vault over a box is not the same as to jump over it, or to get over it somehow or other. Although such terms as 'vault' are not employed in Modern Educational Gymnastics, the same issue of principle applies. There may be greater flexibility in the possibilities of answering a particular task in Educational as compared with more formal gymnastics, yet it is still important to consider how, aesthetically, the task is answered. Clumsy, uncontrolled movements would not be regarded as contributing to an adequate way of answering the task, whichever of the indefinite number of ways may be chosen. Similarly, not any way of dropping into the water would count as a dive. One would have to satisfy at least to a minimal extent the aesthetic requirement built into the meaning of the term for a performance to count as even a bad dive.

The distinction, then, is clear. A purposive sport is one in which, within the rules or conventions, there is an indefinite variety of ways of achieving the end which at least largely defines the game. By contrast, an aesthetic sport is one in which the purpose cannot be specified independently of the manner of achieving it. For instance, it would make no sense to suggest to a figure-skater that it did not matter *how* he performed his movements, as long as he achieved the purpose of the sport, since that purpose inevitably *concerns* the manner of performance. It would make perfectly good sense to urge a football team to score goals without caring how they scored them. Perhaps the point can be made most clearly by reference to the example given above, of the aesthetic norms built into terms such as 'vault' and 'dive', for whereas not *any* way of dropping into the water could count as even a bad dive, *any* way of getting the ball between the opponents' posts, as long as it is within the rules, would count as a goal, albeit a very clumsy or lucky one.

There is a common tendency to distinguish between these two types of sports in terms of competition. For example, in an interesting article on this topic, Reid (1970) distinguishes between what I have called purposive and aesthetic sports in the following way:

> Games come at the end of a kind of spectrum. In most games, competition against an opponent (individual or team) is assumed . . . At the other end of the spectrum there are gymnastics, diving, skating . . . in which grace, the manner in which the activity is carried out, seems to be of central importance.

Against this, I would point out that competition in Olympic gymnastics, skating and diving can be every bit as keen as it can be in Rugby football. Reid is adopting the prevalent but mistaken practice of contrasting the competitive with the aesthetic. Yet, for instance, it is quite apparent that, on occasion, competition between dance companies, and between rival dancers within the same company, can be as intense and as nasty as it can in ice-hockey. Moreover, to take a paradigm case, there are competitive music festivals, in which a similar spirit may be engendered. The great Korean violinist, Kyung-Wha Chung, after winning first prize in one competition, remarked: 'It was one of the worst experiences of my life, because competitions bring out the worst in people.'

CLOSING THE GAP

We can now return to the original question concerning the characterisation of the aesthetic way of looking at sport. By examining the paradigm cases of sports in which the aesthetic is logically inseparable from what the performer is trying to achieve, we might hope to discover aspects of this way of considering them which can be found to apply even to purposive sports, when they are looked at aesthetically.

In figure-skating, diving, synchronised swimming, trampolining and Olympic gymnastics it is of the first importance that there should be no wasted energy and no superfluous movements. Champion gymnasts, like Nadia Comaneçi and Ludmilla Tourischeva, not only perform striking physical feats, but do so with such remarkable economy and efficiency of effort that it often looks effortless. There is an intensive concentration of the gymnast's effort so that it is all directed precisely and concisely onto that specific task. Any irrelevant movement or excessive expenditure of energy would detract from the quality of the performance as a whole, just as superfluous or exaggerated words, words which fail to contribute with maximum compression of meaning to the total effect, detract from the quality of a poem as a whole.

However, even in the case of the aesthetic sports there is still, although no doubt to a very limited extent, an externally identifiable aim; for example the requirements set by each particular movement, and by the particular group of movements, in gymnastics. Now it might be thought that it would be justifiable to regard such stringencies as analogous to, say, the form of a sonnet. That is, it may be thought more appropriate to regard them as setting a framework within which the performer has the opportunity to reveal his expertise in moving gracefully than as an externally identifiable aim. There is certainly something in this notion, but it is significant that there is no analogy in aesthetic sports with poetic licence. The poet may take liberties with the sonnet form without necessarily detracting from the quality of the sonnet, but if the gymnast deviates from the requirements of, for instance, a vault, however gracefully, then that inevitably does detract from the standard of the performance. Nevertheless, the main point for our purposes is that even if, in the aesthetic sports, the means never quite reaches the ultimate of complete identification with the end which is such an important distinguishing feature of the concept of art, it at least closely approximates to such an identification. The gap between means and end is almost, if not quite, completely closed.

Now I want to suggest that the same consideration applies to our aesthetic appreciation of sports of the purposive kind. However successful a sportsman may be in achieving the principal aim of his particular activity, our *aesthetic* acclaim is reserved for him who achieves it with maximum economy and efficiency of effort. We may admire the remarkable stamina and consistent success of an athlete such as Zatopek, but he was not an aesthetically attractive runner because so much of his movement seemed irrelevant to the ideal of most direct accomplishment of the task. The ungainliness of his style was constituted by the extraneous rolls or jerks which seemed wasteful in that they were not concisely aimed at achieving the most efficient use of his energy.

So to consider the purposive sports from the aesthetic point of view is to reduce the gap between means and end. It is, as nearly as possible, to telescope them into the ideal of unity. From a purely purposive point of view any way of winning, within the rules, will do, whereas not *any* way of winning will do as far as aesthetic considerations are concerned. There is a narrower range of possibilities available for the achievement of the end in an aesthetically pleasing way, since the end is no longer simply to win, but to win with the greatest economy and efficiency of effort. Nevertheless, the highest aesthetic satisfaction is experienced and given by the sportsman who not only performs with graceful economy, but who also *achieves* his purpose. The tennis player who serves a clean ace with impeccable style has, and gives to the spectator, far more aesthetic satisfaction than when he fractionally faults with an equally impeccable style. In the case of the purposive sports there is an independently specifiable framework, i.e. one which does not require the sort of judgement to assess achievement which is necessary in the aesthetic sports. Maximum aesthetic success still requires the attainment of the end, and the aesthetic in any degree requires direction onto that end, but the number of ways of achieving such success is reduced in comparison with the purely purposive interest of simply accomplishing the end in an independently specifiable sense.

This characteristic of the aesthetic in activities which are primarily functional also applies to the examples cited earlier of mathematical proofs and philosophical arguments. The proof of a theorem in Euclidean geometry or a philosophical argument is aesthetically pleasing to the extent that there is a clean and concisely directed focus of effort. Any over-elaborate, irrelevant, or repetitious section, in either case, would detract from the maximum economy in achieving the conclusion which gives greatest aesthetic satisfaction. Rhetorical flourishes, however aesthetically effective in other contexts, such as a political speech, detract aesthetically from a philosophical argument by fussily blurring the ideal of a straight, direct line to the conclusion. The aesthetic satisfaction given by rhetoric in a political speech is related to the latter's different purpose of producing a convincing or winning argument rather than a valid one.

The aesthetic pleasure which we derive from sporting events of the purposive kind, such as hurdling and putting the shot, is, then, derived from looking at, or performing, actions which we take to be approaching the ideal of totally concise direction towards the required end of the particular activity. Skiing provides a good example. The stylish skier seems superbly economical, his body automatically accommodating itself, apparently without conscious effort on his part, to the most appropriate and efficient positions for the various types and conditions of terrain. By contrast, the skiing in a slalom race often appears ungainly because it looks forced and less concisely directed. The skier in such an event may achieve greater speed, but only by the expenditure of a disproportionate amount of additional effort. Similarly, athletes at the end of a distance race often abandon the smooth, graceful style with which they have run the greater part of the race. They achieve greater speed but at disproportionate cost, since ungainly, irrelevant movements appear—the head rolls, the body lurches, and so on. In rowing, too, some oarsmen can produce a faster speed with poor style but more, if less effectively produced, power. Even though it is wasteful, the net effective power may still be greater than that of the oarsman who directs his more limited gross power with far more efficiency and therefore with more pleasing aesthetic effect. It is often said that a good big 'un will beat a good little 'un. It is also true in many sports, unfortunately, that a poor big 'un may well beat a far better little 'un.

Perhaps these considerations do something to explain the heightened aesthetic awareness which is achieved by watching slow-motion films and television replays, since (1) we have more time to appreciate the manner of the performance, and (2) the object of the action, the purpose, in an extrinsic sense, becomes less important. That is, our attention is directed more to the character of the action than to its result. We can see whether and how every detail of every movement in the action as a whole contributes to making it the most efficient and economical way of accomplishing that particular purpose. A smooth, flowing style is more highly regarded aesthetically because it appears to require less effort for the same result than a jerky one. Nevertheless, as was mentioned above, achievement of the purpose is still important. However graceful and superbly directed the movements of a pole-vaulter, our aesthetic pleasure in his performance is marred if he knocks the bar off.

One additional and related factor is that some people naturally move gracefully whatever they may be doing, and this may contribute to the aesthetic effect of their actions in sport. If I may be pardoned for the outrageous pun, Muhammad Ali provides a striking example.

Several questions remain. For example, why are some sporting events regarded as less aesthetically pleasing than others, i.e. where we are not comparing actions within the same context of direction onto a common end, but comparing actions in different contexts? For instance, in my view the butterfly stroke in swimming, however well performed, seems less aesthetically pleasing than the crawl. Perhaps this is because it looks less efficient as a way of moving through the water, since there appears to be a disproportionate expenditure of effort in relation to the achievement. A similar example is race walking which, even at its best, never seems to me to be an aesthetically pleasing event. Perhaps, again, this is because one feels that the same effort would be more efficiently employed if the walker broke into a run. In each of these cases one is implicitly setting a wider context, seeing the action in terms of a wider purpose, of movement through water and movement over the ground respectively. But what of a sport such as weight-lifting, which many regard as providing little or no aesthetic pleasure, although it is hard to discover a wider context, a more economical direction on to a wider or similar end in another activity, with which we are implicitly comparing it? Perhaps the explanation lies simply in a general tendency to prefer, from an aesthetic point of view, sports which allow for smooth, flowing movements in the achievement of the primary purpose. Nevertheless, for the devotee, there are, no doubt, 'beautiful' lifts, so called because they accomplish maximum direction of effort.

Now the objection has been made against my account that it fails to differentiate the aesthetic from the skilful. I think two points are sufficient to overcome this objection. First, as a careful reading of the chapter will reveal, my argument, if valid, shows that in sport the two concepts are certainly intimately related, but it also shows that they are not entirely co-extensive. I have marked some ways in which they diverge.

The second and more important point is this. Even if it were true that my argument had not revealed a distinction between the two concepts, that would not constitute an objection to it. For why should not those features of an action in virtue of which it is called skilful also be those in virtue of which it is called aesthetically pleasing? Wittgenstein once wrote: 'Ethics and aesthetics are one.' Whether or not one would want to accept that statement will depend on Wittgenstein's argument for it. One cannot simply dismiss it on the grounds that it *must* be self-defeating to offer a characterisation of the aesthetic which also characterises the ethical.

The supposed objection seems to incorporate the preconception that to have characterised the aesthetic is to have specified those essential features which can be shared by no other concept. This would be like denying that ginger can be an essential ingredient in ginger cakes on the ground that it is *also* an ingredient in ginger ale. The objector produced no argument, but simply assumed that an account which also fitted the skilful could not be adequate as an account of the aesthetic. So, in response to this supposed objection, I could simply reply: 'You are right, I concede that my argument does not entirely distinguish the aesthetic from the skilful. But so far from constituting an objection to my argument, what you have provided amounts to a rough summary of it.'

CONTEXT AND AESTHETIC FEELING

The foregoing argument raises two related considerations which have an important bearing upon the notion of aesthetic *experience* in sport. First, a movement cannot be considered aesthetically in isolation, but only in the context of a particular action in a particular sport. A graceful sweep of the left arm may be very effective in a dance, but the same movement may look ugly and absurd as part of a service action in tennis, or of a pitcher's action in baseball, since it detracts from the ideal of total concentration of effort to achieve the specific task. A specific movement is aesthetically satisfying only if, in the context of the action as a whole, it is seen as forming a unified structure which is regarded as the most economical and efficient method of achieving the required end.

Secondly, there is a danger of serious misconception arising from a mistaken dependence upon feelings as criteria of aesthetic quality, whether in sport or in any other activity, including dance and the other arts. This is part of the misconception to which we alluded in Chapter 6, and consists of taking the feeling of the performer or spectator as the ultimate arbiter. Yet, as we have seen, any feeling is intelligible only if it can be identified by its typical manifestation in behaviour. This is what Wittgenstein (1953) meant by saying that an inner process stands in need of outward criteria. Thus, in the present case, it is the observable physical movement which identifies the feeling and not, as is often believed, the inner feeling which suffuses the physical movement with aesthetic quality or meaning. The feeling could not even be identified if it were not normally experienced in certain objectively recognisable circumstances. One should resist the temptation, commonly encountered in discussion of dance and other forms of movement, to believe that it is how a movement feels which determines its character or effectiveness, whether aesthetic or purposive. That it feels right is no guarantee that it is right. Inexperienced oarsmen in an 'eight' are often tempted to heave their bodies round violently in an attempt to propel the boat more quickly, because such an action gives a feeling of much greater power. Yet in fact it will upset the balance of the boat and thus reduce the effective-ness of the rowing of the crew as a whole. The most effective stroke action can best be judged by the coach who is watching the whole performance from the bank, not by the feeling of the individual oarsmen or even of all the crew. Similarly, in tennis and skiing, to take just two examples, the feeling of an action is often misleading as to its maximum efficiency. A common error in skiing is to lean into the slope and at a certain stage in his progress a learner starts to make turns for the first time which feel very good. Yet, however exhilarating the feeling, if he is leaning the wrong way he will be considerably hampered from making further progress, because in fact he is not directing his efforts in the most effective manner. There are innumerable other such examples one could cite, and this, of course, has important implications for education. If the arbiter of success in physical activities is what the students feel, rather than what they can be observed to do, it is hard to see how such activities can be learned and taught.

However, to refer to an objection which we considered in Chapter 6, it is important not to misunderstand this point by going to the opposite extreme, for I am not saying that we cannot be guided by such feelings, or that they are of no value. My point is that they are useful and reliable only to the extent that they are answerable to patterns of behaviour which can be *observed* to be most efficiently directed onto the particular task. This reveals the connection between this and the preceding point, for it is clear that the character and efficiency of a particular movement cannot be considered in isolation from the whole set of related movements of which it forms a part, and from the purpose towards which they are, as a whole directed. Thus the context in which the movement occurs is a factor of an importance which it is impossible to exaggerate, since the feeling could not even be identified, let alone evaluated, if it were not normally experienced as part of an objectively recognisable action.

In this respect I should like to question what is often said about the aesthetic attitude, namely that it is essentially or predominantly con-templative. Reid (1970), for instance, says: 'In an aesthetic situation we attend to what we perceive in what is sometimes called a "contem-plative" way.' Now it may be that a concern with the arts and the aesthetic is largely contemplative, but I see no reason to deny, indeed I see good reason to insist, that one can have what are most appropriately called aesthetic *feelings* while actually performing an activity. There are numerous examples, such as a well-executed dive, a finely timed stroke in squash, a smoothly accomplished series of movements in gymnastics, an outing in an 'eight' when the whole crew is pulling in unison, with unwavering balance, and a training run when one's body seems to be completely under one's control. For many, the feelings derived from such performances are part of the enjoyment of participation, and 'aesthetic' seems the most appropriate way to characterise them. Reid says that 'a dancer or actor in the full activity of dancing or acting is often, perhaps always, in some degree contemplating the product of his activity'. Later, he says of games players: 'There is no time while the operation is going on to dwell upon aesthetic qualities . . . Afterwards, the participant may look back upon his experience contemplatively with perhaps some aesthetic satisfaction.' Again, of the aesthetic in cricket, he remarks: 'The batsman may enjoy it too, although at the moment of play he has no time to dwell upon it. But to produce exquisite strokes for contemplation is not part of his dominating motive as he is actually engaged in the game . . .' Yet the batsman's aesthetic experience is not necessarily dependent upon his having time at the moment of playing the stroke to 'dwell upon it', nor is it limited to a retrospective contemplation of his performance. If he plays a perfectly timed cover drive with the ball flashing smoothly and apparently effortlessly from the face of his bat to the boundary, the aesthetic satisfaction of the batsman is intrinsic to what he is doing. The aesthetic is not a distinct but perhaps concurrent activity, and it need not depend upon detached or retrospective contemplation. His experience is logically inseparable from the stroke he is playing, in that it is identifiable only by his particular action in that context. And it is quite natural, unexceptionable, and perhaps unavoidable to call such an experience 'aesthetic'. 'Kinaesthetic' or 'tactile' would not tell the whole story by any means, since producing the same physical movement in a quite different context, for instance in a laboratory, could not count as producing the same feeling. Indeed, it is significant that we tend naturally to employ aesthetic terms to describe the feelings involved in such actions. We say that a stroke felt 'beautiful', and it was so to the extent that it was efficiently executed in relation to the specific purpose of the action in the sport concerned. Many participants in physical activities have experienced the exquisite feeling, for instance, of performing a dance or gymnastic sequence, of sailing over the bar in a pole vault, or of accomplishing a fluent series of Christis with skis immaculately parallel. It is difficult to know how to describe these feelings other than as 'aesthetic'. It is certainly the way in which those of us who have taken part in such activities tend spontaneously to refer to them. So, although I do not wish to deny that contemplation is an important part of the aesthetic, I would contend that it is not exhaustive. It is by no means unusual to experience aesthetic feelings, properly so called, while actually engaged and fully involved in physical activities. Moreover, many of us who have derived considerable pleasure from a wide variety of sporting activities would want to insist that such aesthetic experience constitutes a large part of the enjoyment of participation.

THE AESTHETIC AND THE ARTISTIC

In the case of the purposive sports, then, as the actions become more and more directly aimed, with maximum economy and efficiency, at the required end, they become more and more specific, and the gap between means and end is to that extent reduced. That is, increasingly it is less possible to specify the means apart from the end. In these sports the gap will, nevertheless, never be entirely closed in that there cannot be the complete identification of means and end, or more accurately perhaps, the inappropriateness of the distinction between means and end, which obtains in the case of art. For even if in fact there is a single most efficient and economical way of achieving a particular end, this is a contingent matter. The evolution of improved high-jumping methods is a good example. The scissor jump was once regarded as the most efficient method, but it has been overtaken by the straddle, the Western roll and the Fosbury flop.

There remains an interesting question. The aesthetic sports have been shown to be similar to the arts with respect to the impossibility of distinguishing means and ends. Does this mean that such sports can legitimately be regarded as art forms? I should want to insist that they cannot, for two reasons. First, as we have seen, there is good reason to doubt whether the means/end distinction ever quite becomes inappropriate, although it almost reaches that point, even in the aesthetic sports. That is, unlike dance, in these sports there is still an externally specifiable aim even though, for instance, it is impossible entirely to specify what the gymnast is trying to achieve apart from the way in which he is trying to achieve it. Perhaps this is what some physical educationists are getting at when they say, rather vaguely, that a distinction between gymnastics and dance is that the former is objective while the latter is subjective.

However, it is the second reason which is the more important one, and this concerns the distinction which is almost universally overlooked or oversimplified, and therefore misconceived, between the aesthetic and the artistic. The aesthetic applies, for instance, to sunsets, birdsong and mountain ranges, whereas the artistic tends to be limited, at least in its central uses, to artifacts or performances intentionally created by man—*objets trouvés*, if regarded as art, would be so in an extended sense. Throughout this chapter I have so far followed the common practice of taking 'aesthetic' to refer to the genus of which the artistic is a species. My reason for doing so is that any other difference between the two concepts is of no consequence to my main argument, since their logical character with respect to the possibility of distinguishing between means and end is the same. However, in order to consider the question of whether any sport can justifiably be regarded as an art form a more adequate distinction between the aesthetic and the artistic is required, and on examination it becomes clear that there is a much more important issue here than is commonly supposed. I can begin to bring out the issue to which I refer by considering Reid's answer to the question. He is prepared to allow that what I call the aesthetic sports may justifiably be called art, but in my view his conclusion is invalidated because his own formulation of the distinction overlooks a crucial characteristic of art. He writes (1970):

> When we are talking about the category of art, as distinct from the category of the aesthetic, we must be firm, I think, in insisting that in art there is someone who has made (or is making) purposefully an artifact, and that in his purpose there is contained as an essential part the idea of producing an object (not necessarily a 'thing': it could be a movement or a piece of music) in some medium for aesthetic contemplation ... the movement (of a gymnast, skater, diver), carried out in accordance with the general formula, has aesthetic quality fused into it, transforming it into an art quality ... The question is whether the production of aesthetic value is intrinsically part of the purpose of these sports. (If so, on my assumptions, they will be in part, at least, art.)

This certainly has the merit of excluding natural phenomena such as sunsets and roses, but some people might regard his exclusion of *objets trouvés* as somewhat difficult to justify. What, in my view, is worse, this conception would include much which we should be strongly disinclined to call 'art'. For example, a wallpaper pattern is normally designed to give aesthetic pleasure, but it would not on that account, at least in the great majority of cases, be regarded as art. Many such counter-examples spring to mind; for instance the paint on the walls of my office, the shape of radiators and spectacles, and coloured toilet paper. In each case the intention is to give aesthetic pleasure, but none is art (which is not necessarily to deny that, in certain unusual circumstances, any of them could be considered as art, or as part of a work of art).

Reid has done sufficient in my view to show clearly that the great majority of sports cannot legitimately be regarded as art. For the *principal* aim in most sports is certainly not to produce performances for aesthetic pleasure. The aesthetic is incidental. And if it should be argued against me that nevertheless such purposive sports *could* be considered from the aesthetic point of view, my reply would be that so could everything else. Hence, if that were to be regarded as the distinguishing feature of art then *everything* would be art, and thus the term 'art' would no longer have any application.

Nevertheless, Reid's formulation fails, I think, because he overlooks the central aspect of the concept of art which underlies the fact that there are cases where one may appreciate a work of art aesthetically but not artistically. To understand the significance of this point, consider the following example. Some years ago I went to watch a performance by Ram Gopal, the great Indian classical dancer, and I was enthralled by the exhilarating quality of his movements. Yet I did not appreciate, because I could not have understood, his dance artistically, for there is an enormous number of precise meanings given to hand gestures in Indian classical dance, of which I knew none. So it seems clear that my appreciation was of the aesthetic not the artistic.

This example brings out the important characteristic of the concept of art which I particularly want to emphasise, since it is generally overlooked by those who conflate 'aesthetic' and 'artistic'. Moreover, the failure to recognise it is probably the main source of misconceived distinctions between the two terms. I shall first outline the point roughly, and go on to elucidate it more fully in relation to other claims made for sport as art.

It is distinctive of any art form that its conventions allow for the possibility of the expression of a conception of life situations. Thus the arts are characteristically concerned with contemporary moral, social, political and emotional issues. Yet this is not true of the aesthetic. I think it is because he does not recognise the significance of this point that Reid is prepared to allow that the aesthetic sports may legitimately be regarded as art forms. But it is this characteristic of art which is my reason for insisting that even those sports in which the aesthetic is intrinsic, and which are therefore performed to give aesthetic satisfaction, cannot justifiably be considered as art. For in synchronised swimming, figure-skating, diving, trampolining and gymnastics, the performer does not, as part of the convention of the activity, have the possibility of expressing through his particular medium his view of life situations. It is difficult to imagine a gymnast who included in his sequence movements which expressed his view of war, or of love in a competitive society, or of any other such issue. Certainly if he did so it would, unlike art, *detract* to that extent from his performance.

Of course there are cases, even in the accredited arts, such as abstract paintings and dances, where we are urged not to look for a meaning but simply to enjoy the line, colour, movement etc., without trying to read anything into them. But it is intrinsic to the notion of an art form that it can at least *allow for* the possibility of considering issues of social concern, and this is not possible in the aesthetic sports. Incidentally, if I am right that the activities of art and sport are quite distinct, this poses problems for those who suggest that the aesthetic sports may provide one method of, perhaps an introduction to, education in the arts, although of course this is not in the least to cast doubt on their aesthetic value. At their best these sports are undoubtedly superb aesthetically, but they are not, in my view, art.

SPORT AND ART

Partly in order to bring out more fully the important characteristic of the concept of art which I have just outlined, and partly because of the widespread misconception on the issue, I should like further to elucidate my reasons for denying the common supposition that sport can legitimately be considered as art.

As we have seen, it is clear that there is a distinction between the aesthetic and the artistic, even though it may be difficult precisely to delineate it. Yet, in the literature on sport, one still very frequently encounters an illicit slide from such terms as 'beautiful' and 'graceful' to 'art'. An author will refer to a general interest in the beauty of the movement in various sporting activities, and will assume implicitly or explicitly that this entitles such activities to be considered as art. Anthony (1968) and Reid (1970) give several examples, and the same confusion runs through Carlisle (1969) who writes, for instance, that 'various forms of dance are accepted as art forms and aesthetic criteria are also applied in other activities e.g. ice-skating, diving, Olympic gymnastics and synchronised swimming'. A more recent example is Lowe (1976) who writes: 'By analysing dance, as one of the performing arts, with the object of deducing the aesthetic components . . . a step will be taken closer to the clarification of the beauty of sport as a performing art.' So far as I can understand this, Lowe seems to be guilty of the confusion to which I refer, since clearly 'beauty' and its cognates do not necessarily imply 'art'. To say that a young lady is beautiful is not to say that she is a work of art.

For the reasons already given, I submit that, despite the amount of literature on the topic, we should finally abandon this persistent but misguided attempt to characterise sport *in general* as art. Quite apart from what seems to me the obvious misconception involved, I just do not see why it should be thought that sport would somehow be endowed with greater respectability if it could be shown to be art.

There is, of course, a much more convincing case to be made for the credentials of the aesthetic sports as art, although even here I do not think it succeeds. My rejection of the case hinges on the way I have characterised the distinction between the aesthetic and the artistic. It would seem that any attempt to draw this distinction in terms of definition, or by reference to particular kinds of objects or performances, is almost certainly doomed to failure. Hence I distinguish the two concepts by drawing attention to a characteristic which is central to any legitimate art *form*, rather than to a work of art within that medium. Thus, to repeat the point, my own formulation is that any art form, properly so-called, must at least *allow for* the possibility of the expression of a conception of life issues, such as contemporary moral, social and political problems. Such a possibility is an *intrinsic* part of the concept of art, by which I mean that without it an activity could not count as a legitimate art form. It is certainly a crucial factor in the ways in which the arts have influenced society. Examples abound. For instance, it is reported that during the occupation of France in the war a German officer, indicating the painting *Guernica*, asked Picasso, 'Did you do that?' To which Picasso replied, 'No, you did.'

By contrast, such a possibility is not intrinsic to any sport. However, this point has been misunderstood, as a result of which it has been argued against me that in sport, too, there can be comment on life issues. The commonest example cited was that of black American athletes on the rostrum at the Olympic Games, who gave the clenched-fist salute for Black Power during the playing of the national anthem. But this does not constitute a counter-example, since such a gesture is clearly *extrinsic* to, not made from within, the conventions of sport as such. The conventions of art are in this respect significantly different from those in sport, since it is certainly intrinsic to art that a view could be expressed, for instance on colour discrimination, as in Athol Fugard's plays about the issue in South Africa.

We have seen that since aesthetic terms such as 'beauty' are often applied to sport, it is sometimes erroneously supposed that therefore sport is art. A similar misconception occurs with respect to the terms 'dramatic', 'tragic', and their cognates. These terms are used in a notoriously slippery way, hence it certainly cannot be assumed that they are used in other contexts as they are in art. For instance, if I were to leap up during a meeting, shout abusive terms, and hurl a cup through a window, that would certainly be dramatic, but I am modest enough to assume that no one would regard it as artistic.

It is an understood part of the convention that tragedy in a play happens to the *fictional characters* being portrayed, and not to the actors, i.e. the living people taking part. By contrast, and ignoring for a moment the issue of whether it would be legitimately employed in such a context, 'tragedy' in sport *does* happen to the participants, i.e. to the living people taking part. For example, let us imagine that I am playing the part of Gloucester, in the play *King Lear*. In the scene where his eyes are put out it is agonising for the character in the play,

Gloucester; not for me, the actor. There is no comparable convention in sport such that it would make sense to say of a serious injury in Rugby that it occurred to the full-back, and not to the man who was playing full-back. While in Canada recently I was given an interesting illustration of the point. A party of Eskimos, attending a performance of *Othello*, were appalled to see what they took to be the killing of people on the stage. They had to be reassured by being taken back-stage after the performance to see the actors still alive. The Eskimos had assumed that different actors would be required for each performance.

To put the point roughly, it is a central convention of art, in contrast to sport, that the object of one's attention is an *imagined* object. Thus a term such as 'tragic', used of art, has to be understood as deriving its meaning from that convention. Yet, although this is a central convention of art, it is overlooked or misconstrued by most of those who argue that sport is art, or drama. This omission vitiates a good deal of the literature on the topic. Reid (1970) gives several examples, including that of Maheu, who claims that 'spectator sports are the true theatre of our day'; Carlisle (1969) who supports the contention that cricket is 'an art form both dramatic and visual'; Kitchin, who in an article on 'Sport as drama' writes of international soccer: 'This is the authentic theatre in the round, from which Hungary's Manager made a thirty-yard running exit with both hands clenched over his eyes ... Soccer is drama without a script.' Similarly, Keenan (1973) in an article entitled 'The athletic contest as a "tragic" form of art', writes: 'There is no doubt that athletic contests, like other human endeavours, provide drama. No one would question whether Bannister's effort which produced the first sub-four minute mile was dramatic.' But I would seriously question whether, indeed I would deny that, 'dramatic' is being used here in the same sense as when it occurs in the context of discussion of a play, since the relevant convention is lacking. That there is no comparable convention in sport can be brought out most clearly by the lack of any analogue with a fictional character. What happens to Gloucester does not happen to the person playing the part of Gloucester. The analogue in sport would have to be something like: 'What happened to Hungary's Manager did not happen to the man who held the position as manager', and 'What happened to the athlete who completed the first sub-four-minute mile did not happen to Bannister, who took part in the race', both of which are palpably absurd.

There are two common uses of the term 'tragic' which are outside, and which therefore should not be confused with its use within, the conventions of drama:

(1) Where the term is used, for instance, of serious injury to a

sportsman, the analogue in a play would be serious injury to an actor, for example in an accident during a duelling scene. 'Tragic' in this sense does not depend on conventions at all, whether sporting or artistic, but is used to refer to a poignantly sad and distressing event in real life, such as a seriously crippling or fatal accident or illness.

(2) On the other hand, in the irritatingly prevalent but barbarously debased sense of the term where 'tragic' is used, for instance, of the failure of a sportsman to achieve a success on which he had set his heart, the analogue in drama would be not some tragic event in a play but, for instance, the failure of an actor in a crucial role, or his failure to obtain a role which he earnestly wanted. It is still quite different from the use of the term within the conventions of drama. Strangely enough, Keenan (1973) recognises this point to some extent, yet fails to realise that it undermines his whole case. He writes: 'We can truly sympathise with classic efforts of athletic excellence that end in tragedy. They parallel the difficult episodes in life.' As one example, he cites an Olympic marathon race:

> The amazing Pietri entered the stadium with an enormous lead on the field, needing only to negotiate the last 385 yards to win. His effort had left him in an obvious state of extreme physical fatigue ... The crowd cheered lustily for him to continue, to fight off the fatigue, to win. His final collapse came near the finish line as the eventual winner ... was just entering the stadium.

This example, so far from supporting Keenan's case reveals the fatal flaw in it, for 'tragedy' here is used in the latter sense adumbrated above, and is totally different from the way the term is used within and as part of the conventions of drama. The point can be brought sharply into focus by recognising that a poignantly tragic moment in drama is a *triumph*, a mark of *success*, for an actor, whereas, by contrast a 'tragic' moment in sport is a *failure*, even if a noble and courageous failure, for the competitor.

The importance of the conventions of art can be brought out in another way, by reference to the use of the term 'illusion'. In the context of the arts 'illusion' is not employed as it would be of, for instance, a mirage. One actually, if mistakenly, believes that an oasis is there, whereas one does not actually believe that someone is being murdered on a stage. Or at least, if one should actually believe that someone is being murdered this significantly reveals a failure to grasp one of the most important conventions of drama. The term 'illusion' is used in a different, if related, sense in the context of art. I say that the sense is related because, for instance, the actors, theatre management and producer, by means of lighting, stage effects and a high standard of acting, try to induce the audience to suspend their disbelief, as it were. Nevertheless, as Scruton (1974) puts it, our experience of representation and expression in art 'derives from imagination, not belief'.

Of course this is not in the least to deny that it is possible to be imaginative in sport, although I have been rather surprisingly misunderstood in this respect. What it does deny is that there are analogous conventions in sport such that the participants have to be imagined, as one has to imagine the characters in a play or novel.

In short, the misconception of those writers who persist in what I firmly believe are misguided attempts to argue that sport is an art form, stems from their ignoring or misconstruing the crucial importance of the *art* aspect of a work of art. For instance, one commonly experiences emotional responses to both artistic and sporting performances, and as both spectator and performer. Now, emotional feelings can be identified only by criteria, of which the most important is what is called the 'intensional object', i.e. the kind of object towards which the emotion is directed. In the case of art, the intensional object cannot be characterised in isolation from the relevant conventions. The point becomes particularly clear, perhaps, when we think how we can be moved by completely non-naturalistic works of art, such as surrealism, abstract expressionism, and an allegory such as *Le Petit Prince* by St-Exupéry.

Now of course with respect to sport, too, the intensional object cannot be characterised independently of the conventions of that particular kind of activity. The point was brought home vividly to me when for the first time I watched an American Football match, which was a keenly contested local derby between two rival high schools. There was considerable partisan excitement, but I was unable to share in it because I did not understand the game. As an even clearer example, a friend in Jasper told me of his experience, while working in the North West Territories, of trying to teach the local Eskimos how to play soccer. He was frustrated, apparently, by their inability to understand, or at least refusal to accept, that the purpose of the game was to defeat the opposing team. The Eskimos were much too genial to adopt such an uncivilised, competitive ethos, hence if a team were winning, members of it would promptly score in their own goal in order to be generous to their opponents.

So one certainly needs to understand the conventions of sport, too, in order to become emotionally involved in the appropriate way. But the conventions of sport are in important respects very different from those of art, even in the case of aesthetic sports such as figure-skating. The champion skater John Curry has strongly expressed his conviction that figure-skating *should* be regarded as an art form, and the superb Canadian skater, Toller Cranston, is frequently quoted as a counter-example by Canadians. He, too, apparently, has often insisted that figure-skating is an art. However, this contention is based on a confusion, and in my opinion it would be clearer to conceive of them as two quite distinct kinds of activity. Then we should have on one hand the *sport* of figure-skating, and on the other hand the *art* of modern dance on ice, which these skaters want to create as a new art form. It is interesting that Toller Cranston is said to have expressed annoyance at the limitations imposed by the conventions and rules of the *sport*, and has made his point forcefully by *deliberately* performing his figure-skating in several competitions *as* an art form. For instance, in response to the music he had flouted the canons of the sport by performing movements which *did* express his view of life situations. But it is significant that, much to his further chagrin, he *lost* marks for doing so. In my view the judges were quite right. The context of sport, even an aesthetic sport, is not appropriate for art. It is significant, perhaps, and tacitly concedes my point, that John Curry has put his convictions into practice by creating 'The John Curry Theatre of Skating'.

Now it might be objected that in denying in this way that sport can legitimately be regarded as art I am simply being stipulative. That is, it might be said that this is arbitrarily to lay down how the term 'art' should be used. This objection is of the same kind as that which was discussed in Chapter 4 with respect to the use of 'intellectual', and it can be met in a similar way. Certainly philosophers cannot legislate how words should be used, and what is to count as correct usage. 'Artistic' could be used as synonymous with 'aesthetic', and there could be no *philosophical* objection to what I regard as barbarously degenerate uses such as 'the art of cooking'. The philosophical point is that, however the term may be used, this will not *remove*, even although it may blur, the relevant distinction. That is, if 'art' were to be used as broadly as this, there would still be a distinction between those forms of activity which have, and those which do not have, intrinsic to their conventions, the possibility of comment on life issues in the way described. And in such a case, it would be necessary to employ some other term to mark those which have this kind of convention. Hence it seems to me much less conducive to confusion to restrict 'art' to such activities.

To repeat the point, then, in my opinion it is high time we buried once for all the prolix attempts to show that sport is art. It may be of interest to point up illuminating similarities, but only confusion can accrue from the attempt to equate the two kinds of activity. In the case of an aesthetic sport such as figure-skating the suggestion is at least initially plausible because of the widespread failure to recognise the important distinction between the aesthetic and the artistic, and because figure-skating, unlike, for instance, football, can so easily become an art form. But in the case of the purposive sports, which constitute the great majority, there is not even a *prima facie* case, even though there may be many movements in such sports which are superb aesthetically.

Rather ironically, the fact that sporting activities and the movements of athletes have been the subject for art, for instance in painting and sculpture, is sometimes adduced, at least by implication, in support of the contention that sport is art. For example, Lowe (1976) writes:

Among sculptors, R. Tait McKenzie has brought a fine sense of movement to his athletic studies cast in bronze. There is no question about the aesthetic qualities of these art works: hence they provide intrinsic clues to our grasp of the elusive nature of beauty in sport.

I say that it is ironic because examination reveals that this kind of argument achieves the very opposite of what its authors intend, since it makes the point which could also be regarded as a summary of my distinction between the aesthetic and the artistic. For whereas sport can be the subject of art, art could not be the subject of sport. Indeed, the very notion of a *subject* of sport makes no sense.

REFERENCES: CHAPTER 7

Anthony, W. J., 'Sport and physical education as a means of aesthetic education', *British Journal of Physical Education*, vol. 60, no. 179 (March 1968).

Bambrough, J. R., 'To reason is to generalise', *The Listener*, vol. 89, no. 2285 (11 January 1973).

Best, D., *Expression in Movement and the Arts* (London: Lepus Books, Henry Kimpton Publishers, 1974).

Carlisle, R., 'The concept of physical education', *Proceedings of the Philosophy of Education Society of Great Britain*, vol. 3 (January 1969).

Keenan, F., 'The athletic contest as a "tragic" form of art', in *The Philosophy of Sport*, ed. R. G. Osterhoudt (Springfield, Illinois: C. C. Thomas, 1973).

Lowe, B., 'Toward scientific analysis of the beauty of sport', *British Journal of Physical Education*, vol. 7, no. 4 (July 1976).

Reid, L. A., 'Sport, the aesthetic and art', *British Journal of Educational Studies*, vol. 18, no. 3 (1970).

Scruton, R., *Art and Imagination* (London: Methuen, 1974).

Wittgenstein, L., *Philosophical Investigations* (Oxford: Basil Blackwell, 1953).

Chapter 8

Meaning in Movement

INTRODUCTION

It is generally assumed that language is symbolic. In this chapter we shall consider the widely accepted theory that symbolism is also the explanation of the meaning of the various forms of human movement. It will be argued that implicit in such a theory are forms of dualism which reduce it to unintelligibility. Perhaps the most important of these is a seminal, underlying misunderstanding of the nature of the conceptualisation given with language, and its relationship with reality.

Eleanor Metheny's book *Connotations of Movement in Sport and Dance* (1965) will be used as a stalking horse for three principal reasons: (1) because it is so thoroughly worked out; (2) because it so clearly manifests the three forms of dualism which are to be examined; and (3) because it is so well known among those in the field of human movement and physical education. Her later book (1968) will not be considered because in my view it is not so thoroughly worked out, and anyway reveals no change in her general position.

SYMBOLISM

Metheny clearly assumes that there must be some single way of characterising the meaning of movement. Although this is a tempting notion, those engaged in the study of human movement should, perhaps, be more aware than most people of the varied character of the movements in the relevant activities, and therefore should be aware of the possibility of commensurately varied kinds of meaning. However, this assumption, together with a common misconception about linguistic meaning, lead her to propose the thesis that meaning is necessarily symbolic, and thus that a word or movement has meaning only by symbolising. She makes a clear statement of this general thesis by reference to linguistic meaning:

> Speech . . . is the most obvious example of man's ability to express symbolic meanings in coherent and well-articulated terms. In speaking, he uses vocalized sounds to symbolize the connection he finds between a concept of an event and the event as such.

If taken literally this is difficult to understand. For it is unclear how the vocalised sounds are supposed to symbolise the *connection* between concept and event. I shall assume that this is a slip, and that Metheny means that the sounds symbolise the concept of the event.

There is a common and unquestioned assumption that language is symbolic in that the words which comprise it have symbolic meanings, yet in fact the assumption is highly questionable. It may be plausible to suggest that words like 'table', 'flower', and verbal phrases like 'Sir Winston Churchill' are endowed with meaning by standing for or symbolising something. But what does the word 'if' symbolise? What does 'and' stand for? What about 'then', 'or', 'as' and 'most'? One can readily think of many more examples which would severely strain the theory. Even the more plausible examples involve considerable difficulties. For instance, what, precisely, does the word 'table' symbolise? Is it this or that table, all tables, or any conceivable table? There is an oddity in maintaining that the word stands for any table since, for instance, it would have to stand for tables which have not yet even been made. Moreover, how is it that a group of letters 'table', or the sound made by uttering the word 'table', can symbolise a physical object? There is no obvious similarity between them, so how does one symbolise the other? But there is another, more obviously fatal, objection which can be raised, for if the meaning of the words 'Sir Winston Churchill' were entirely dependent on their symbolising the man, Sir Winston Churchill, then, according to the theory, those words should now be meaningless, since Sir Winston Churchill is dead. Yet clearly the meaning of the words is not dead since they can be intelligibly used.

A more plausible version of the theory, adopted by Metheny, supposes that the words symbolise not the man himself but the idea or concept of the man, which can certainly survive the man's death. This version will be considered more carefully in a moment, but it will be recalled from Chapter 1 that it incurs equally intractable difficulties. To put the point briefly, if the meaning of a verbal term were to depend upon an inner mental idea or concept, it would be incomprehensible. For instance, since, according to the theory, such ideas are inaccessibly private, it is obviously absurd to suggest that I could somehow examine the idea symbolised in your mind by the words 'Sir Winston Churchill' in order to discover whether it corresponded with the idea symbolised in my mind. Since this would apply equally to the meaning of every word used by everyone, no sense could be given to the notions of language, meaning and communication. Indeed, its proponents are not even entitled to formulate the theory in these terms since according to their own thesis there could be no *words* but only incomprehensible sounds or marks. Thus, ironically, if the theory were correct it could not even be stated.

Metheny's preconception that the meaning of human movement must also be explicable in terms of symbolism is revealed in the following statement about sports competition: 'Men attach great value to this seemingly futile effort. It would seem, therefore, that this behavioural form must symbolize some more significant conception of man's interaction with the universe of his existence.' The word 'must' used in this way is frequently significant, in that it suggests that a theory is being imposed inflexibly, albeit perhaps inadvertently, upon every relevant situation considered, with the result that possible counter-instances may be overlooked or misconstrued in order to fit the theory. One should be on one's guard against this tendency, to which we are all prone, for it is often difficult to recognise that one is so immersed in a theory that one is distorting features of a situation which ought instead to strike one as requiring a reconsideration of that theory. This is rather like being so incapable of questioning the accuracy of one's map that on finding a discrepancy one insists that it must be the landscape which is mistaken.

No doubt as a consequence of a similar inability seriously to question her assumption that meaning is necessarily symbolic, Metheny takes her view to extraordinary lengths. For example, she writes that modern Olympic Games 'may well symbolize man's conception of himself as a consequential force within the grand design of the universe, as well as each man's conception of his own ability to perform those functions that identify him as a man among men'. It is difficult to make much sense of this, but as far as I am able to understand it, such a notion would apply equally to almost if not quite every other activity and achievement of human beings, such as playing the organ, hairdressing, renovating a bathroom and baking potatoes.

The general misconception about symbolism is in an important respect similar to that of definitions. A is defined in terms of B; C symbolises D. In each case one entity or activity is explained by reference to another, and the explanation is regarded as fully successful only if the latter *comprehensively* characterises the former. But on reflection this strikes one as an oddly implausible notion in general, for if every entity or activity can be comprehensively characterised in terms of another, there must be an enormous amount of duplication in the universe. Wittgenstein (1953) aptly referred to this kind of misconception as the tendency to regard everything as a diminished version of itself.

DUALISM 1: INNER THOUGHT//OVERT BEHAVIOUR

Let us now consider the precise formulation of Metheny's theory. If I understand her correctly, it can be expressed schematically in this way:

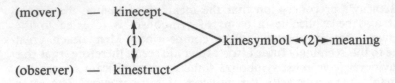

The kinecept is the inner thought or experience of the mover, and the kinestruct is the overt expression of it in observable movement. As Metheny puts it:

> For the mover, the meaning of the movement is conceptualised in the kinesymbolic form of the kinecept. His overt movement is a kinesymbolic expression of that meaning in the form of a kinestruct ... The meanings the mover expresses and the meanings understood by the observer are probably never identical. Each person interprets symbolic forms within his own frame of reference.

There are two closely related problems of dualism implicit in this theory: (1) the relationship between the kinecept and the kinestruct, i.e. what could possibly justify the assertion that a particular, or indeed any, inner thought or experience *is* being overtly expressed in a particular movement; and (2) the relationship between the kinesymbol and the meaning, i.e. what could possibly justify the assertion that the inner experience (kinecept) or overt movement (kinestruct) *does* symbolise a particular, or indeed any, meaning. In schematic formulation again:

Dualism 1: kinecept (inner thought or experience)   (?) kinestruct (overt movement)

Dualism 2: kinesymbol   (?) meaning

The question marks indicate the logical problem in each case, and 1 and 2 are, of course, the same as in the schema above.

Let us first examine dualism 1. It is clear from the quotation above and from many statements she makes that Metheny assumes a general dualist theory of body and mind. For example, she says that a symbolic form formulates meaning, and goes on: 'In its private form, as a thought, concept or idea, it is comprehended only by the person who is thinking it; in its public form, it is an expression of that thought or meaning.' What largely contributes to this fundamental misconception is a radically confused, if common, notion of meaning as a sort of inner mental idea or image which is formed by the experiences one undergoes. She *says* that she is aware of the difference between what she calls 'connotation' and meaning, but in fact she conflates them, with disastrous consequences. For example, she states that the meaning of a kinesymbol is a complex of connotations. It would be too much of a diversion to consider the question of the various meanings of 'meaning' in the detail it merits, but it is easy to show that Metheny has failed to notice an important distinction in her theory. Certainly there is a sense of the term which is used to ask a question such as 'What does X mean to you?' But this sense is roughly equivalent to 'What is the significance of X to you?', and is completely different from questions about the meaning of X. In the former sense there is an indefinitely wide range of answers to each such question. For example, in response to the question 'What does Rugby football mean to you?' there are various possible answers, such as 'An opportunity to work out of my system the frustrations of the week'; 'An opportunity to escape from the wife for a few hours'; 'The way Wales can humiliate England'; or even 'Legalised hooliganism'. But none of these answers has anything to do with the meaning, in the *logical* sense, of the term 'Rugby football'. Metheny is confusing the associations of a word or movement with its meaning.

Clearly one may form various associations with a word which are quite irrelevant to its meaning, as we saw in Chapter 5 with respect to the word 'dentist'. To cite another example, the ugly word 'aesthetician' puts me in mind of a practitioner of one of the more recondite branches of medicine—paediatrician, obstetrician, and with pills to cure painful philosophical problems about the arts, aesthetician. And my imagination ran riot when, as an undergraduate, I first encountered some of the more turgid terminological excrescences of academic philosophy, such as 'supererogation' and 'syncategorematic'. Yet obviously such bizarre imaginings have nothing whatsoever to do with the meanings of the terms. That is, connotation, association, or significance should be clearly distinguished from 'meaning' in the logical sense.

The inevitable subjective tendencies implicit in Metheny's conflation of connotation with logical meaning are clearly revealed in this quotation: 'Similar kinestructs may have very different intellectual-emotional import as kinesymbols for different people, their meaning being related to all the reactions ... that occurred within the context of many different situations.' One encounters all too frequently variations of this extraordinary misconception, usually in the form of the assertion that the meaning of words is a purely personal, subjective matter. Sometimes, for instance, the notion is adduced in order to evade uncomfortable philosophical analysis. Someone says: 'Well, that may be your meaning of the word, but it's not what it means to me.' Humpty Dumpty, in *Alice through the*

Looking Glass, amply illustrates the absurdity of such a contention:

'There's glory for you!'
'I don't know what you mean by "glory"', Alice said. Humpty Dumpty smiled contemptuously. 'Of course you don't—till I tell you. I meant there's a nice knock-down argument for you!'
'But "glory" doesn't mean "a nice knock-down argument"', Alice objected.
'When *I* use a word', Humpty Dumpty said in rather a scornful tone, 'it means just what I choose it to mean—neither more nor less'.

Certainly this is a different form of subjectivism. On the 'inner idea' theory *no* word can have an intelligible meaning, whereas it is possible to have an intelligible idiosyncratic meaning for *some* words while depending upon the *general* objectivity of language. But if the idiosyncratic thesis were generalised to apply to *every* word, then it would degenerate to the subjectivism of the 'inner idea' kind, since *no* word could be understood by anyone else. Indeed, as we have seen, the supposition that *every* word could have a purely subjective meaning, understandable only by the person using it, incurs the ironic consequence that the supposition *itself* could not be stated, as it would be incomprehensible. For, of course, it is necessary to *presuppose* an objective, generally understood meaning for the words which one employs even to explain idiosyncratic associations, connotations, or significance. The point is clearly exemplified by Humpty Dumpty who, despite his contemptuous insistence to the contrary, inevitably has to rely on meanings which are *not* chosen in order to explain the abnormal case when he does choose.

Metheny makes a similar assumption about the meaning of dance: 'Every man's analogies are his own, and no one can say "what a dance really means".' Such a notion is equally self-destructive and invalidates her whole enterprise, since it incurs the consequence that dance too would be entirely subjective and thus there could never be any grounds for attributing *any* meaning to it. Certainly no sense could be made of the supposition that it has symbolic meaning.

A precisely similar, fundamental misconception about subjective meaning runs through Phenix (1964). For example, he explains the meaning of dance movements as 'objectifications of inner experiences having *universal import*' (my italics). but since they are, according to the theory itself, inaccessibly private, what possible justification could there be for supposing such inner experiences to have universal or any import, or even to exist? For a consequence of the theory would be that no sense could be given to the notion of any meaning in dance, since it would be impossible to discover whether it did objectify a particular or any inner experience. Metheny assumes that this problem can be overcome by appeal to the notion of inference, i.e. she supposes that we *infer* the thoughts or experiences of others by interpreting their overt physical behaviour. But such a supposition is unintelligible. The *grounds* for a legitimate inference could be given *only* by an observed regular correlation of the relevant events in the past. Yet clearly, in terms of this kind of theory, no sense could be given to the notion of having established a correlation between overt behaviour and inaccessibly private inner thoughts.

It is crucial to understand the *nature* of this objection, and therefore just how radically it undermines the very common kind of theory under consideration. The point can be brought out in this way. In the quotation given above, Metheny wrote: 'The meanings the mover expresses and the meanings understood by the observer are *probably* never identical. Each person interprets symbolic forms within his own frame of reference' (my italics). This reveals how completely she fails to understand the character of the problem. For it is a *logical* problem, and thus to pose it in terms of probability is incoherent. To formulate the difficulty in that way is to conceive of it on the model of an *empirical* difficulty, i.e. as if it could possibly be overcome to some extent by great effort or ingenuity. This, again, is precisely the fundamental confusion inherent in the way in which some phenomenologists conceive of the difficulty of attempting to communicate private, subjective experience. They also seem to think that it requires a great effort of concentration, sensitivity and verbal facility in order to capture and convey, at least to some extent, the elusive character of subjective, inner experience. But to suppose the difficulty to be of that kind is as misconceived as it would be to suppose that great effort and ingenuity would be required to construct a four-sided triangle. For the problem of this kind of theory is not just that the supposed subjective meaning and the interpretation of overt behaviour are *probably* never identical, or that one can never be quite *certain* that they coincide, but, much more radically, that such a theory is able to provide *no grounds whatsoever* for probability or certainty. That is, to propose the difficulty in Metheny's terms makes it sound as if there were something one could not quite *achieve*, whereas, on this model, nothing could possibly *count* as the same meaning. Thus the hypothesis makes as little sense as the supposition that it is probable, or almost certain, that no one will ever succeed in constructing a four-sided triangle.

So, to formulate the point in terms of Metheny's theory, nothing could possibly count as the expression of a kinecept in the overt form of a kinestruct.

Although this kind of theory is a form of dualism, it should be noticed that there is no place at all for any kind of objectivity. *All* meaning is entirely private and subjective. The meaning to be expressed is supposed to be a *subjective* experience or thought. But equally, the overt behaviour or sound has to be interpreted within the observer's *subjective* 'frame of reference'. So, although it is difficult to find a coherent way of formulating the point, the dualism amounts to two forms of subjectivism. The person expressing, and the person interpreting, are each incarcerated in a totally private world of which no one else could possibly know anything.

What makes such theories of subjective meaning and experience so dangerously plausible is that their inevitable and illicit trading on a whole background of *objective* and publicly understood language is overlooked, even by their proponents. This inevitable reliance on objectivity is most apparent, perhaps, from the point I have made several times that without it the subjectivists could not even intelligibly propose their thesis. Further clear indications of this surreptitious, if inadvertent, dependence upon the objectivity supposedly excluded by their own thesis are provided by Metheny's assertion that the meanings of mover and observer are *'probably'* never identical, and Phenix's illegitimate appeal to the *'universal import'* of inner experiences. To assume that a term or movement expresses 'universal import' is to help himself to the objective meaning to which he is not entitled by the terms of his own theory. That is, the fundamental confusion of any such subjective theory is that it inevitably has *implicitly* to rely on precisely the objectivity of meaning which it is *explicitly* trying to deny. It tries to saw off the branch on which it is sitting.

In order to bring out the point in another way I shall freely adapt an example given by Wittgenstein (1953). Suppose that each of a group of people has a box with something in it which is called a 'froonwappa'. No one can look into anyone else's box, and everyone says he knows what a froonwappa is *only* by looking at *his own* froonwappa. It would obviously be possible for everyone to have something quite different in his box. Indeed it might even be constantly changing. The thing in the box clearly can have no place in the language at all; not even as a *something*, for a box might even be empty, i.e. 'a froonwappa' might mean 'an empty space'. Thus one can 'divide through' by the thing in the box; it cancels out, whatever it is.

I hope this discussion will reveal the incoherence of the notion of subjective meaning, often manifested, for example, in phenomenological writing. Such subjective assumptions are only too prevalent in the literature on human movement, and perhaps especially on dance.

It should be mentioned that I have not explicitly raised an even more damaging objection, although it is implicit in much that I have said, namely that no sense at all can be given to the notion of purely private, subjective meaning, even for the person *himself*. There are powerful arguments which show that the notion of meaning, even in one's own case, necessarily depends upon a public, objective language, with implicit rules, and therefore that the supposition of a *private* language, with purely subjective meaning, is incoherent. To pursue those arguments would take us into deep waters, but that is unnecessary since enough has been said to refute the suggestion that subjective meaning could be comprehensible.

One further point should, perhaps, be made in order to avoid a common misunderstanding. It should not be thought that these arguments against subjective meaning imply that thought or experience is impossible unless it is expressed in an observable way. But if the somewhat misleading picture of inner and outer be retained, it is less conducive to error to regard the direction of travel as the opposite to that supposed by subjectivists. For meaning, whether of thoughts, feelings or movements, can be identified only by publicly recognisable criteria, as we saw in Chapter 6 with respect to the experience of the performer. However, this is not to deny, for instance, that someone could have feelings if he were to grow up alone from infancy on a desert island. Although he would have no language he could certainly have feelings. But he would be incapable of knowing *what* feelings they were, or even that they *were* feelings. He would simply feel something. When one has learned to identify a feeling by reference to external behaviour then it can be recognised when it recurs, and, of course, it is not necessary to express it overtly in order to do so.

DUALISM 2: MEANING//MEDIUM OF EXPRESSION

We can now turn to the second form of dualism implicit in Metheny's theory. It is so closely connected with the former that the two are not altogether distinguishable, both in her writing and in the popular misconception about meaning in general. Nevertheless, it is possible to conceive of meaning as logically independent of observable medium of expression without necessarily regarding it as private and subjective.

Metheny clearly conceives of the movement and the meaning as two distinct entities. On the one hand there is the physical movement (kinecept or kinestruct), and on the other hand the meaning of which it is a symbol. She regards meaning as some sort of metaphysical entity which she calls 'feeling about life', which can be made articulate through an observable medium of expression. But such a supposition is incoherent, since nothing could possibly count as the coinciding or correlation of the two entities. That is, no sense could be made of the suggestion that a particular kinecept or kinestruct is a kinesymbol of a particular or any meaning. To put the point another way, since, on Metheny's theory, the meaning entity is supposed to exist prior to and independently of its expression in an objective, observable physical form, the notion that anything could be known of its nature or even of whether it exists at all is unintelligible.

To employ the terminology of symbolism carries a clear implication of dualism, namely the symbol and that which is symbolised. As we have seen, Metheny explicitly accepts that implication with respect to language, in that she clearly regards concepts as independent 'thought' entities which are translated into words so that they can be communicated to other people. This is a common misconception. The notion is that one first has the idea and then, as it were, casts about for a medium in which to express it. Yet, on the supposition that the idea or thought is logically distinct from the medium in which it is expressed, it would be impossible ever to know that a physical medium, such as language or dance, expressed a particular or *any* idea or thought. This issue was considered in Chapter 7 with respect to the problem of form and content in the arts. As we saw then, no sense can be given to the notion of the purpose of, or what is expressed in, a work of art apart from the work of art itself. That is, there is a *logical* relation between meaning and medium of expression, hence no sense could be made of the supposition that the *same* meaning could be expressed in a different work of art.

Metheny, in common with many people, seems to regard it as intelligible to suggest that one could think without *any* medium of expression. On such a view it would make sense to suppose an owl to be capable of profound philosophical thought even though it so happens that he has not yet learned the language in which to express it. Yet, however wise owls may be in fable, such a supposition is incoherent, since without the requisite ability to use language nothing could *count* as having the ability for profound philosophical thought. It would be similarly incoherent to suggest that someone could have a choreographic idea if he did not have the requisite understanding of the art of dance. It is radically misconceived to regard thought or meaning as quite independent of any medium of physical expression.

I hope I shall not be misunderstood as denying that movements can be symbolic. Obviously they can. What I am denying is first, that movements are always and necessarily symbolic, and it is this which uniquely endows them with meaning; and second, that an objectively observable physical medium of expression can intelligibly be supposed to symbolise what is not in principle answerable to sense-perception.

DUALISM 3: LANGUAGE//REALITY

The principal reason for this critical analysis of Eleanor Metheny's theory of meaning and of the common misconceptions it exemplifies is to show that clarity on these issues is a necessary precondition for the proposal of any coherent thesis about the various meanings of human behaviour. To consider the most important of these misconceptions, which is probably the source of the others, will take us back to the most fundamental question of philosophy, which was briefly discussed in Chapter 1, namely the relation of language or conceptualisation to reality. Again, it will be impossible to consider this issue in the depth it merits, but enough can be said to expose the misconception in question, and to outline a coherent account.

Metheny has already been quoted as stating that words and movements symbolise the connection between the concept of an event and the event as such. This sentence reveals precisely the fundamental misconception about the conceptualisation given with language to which I advert. Metheny says that language and symbolic movement 'conceptualise' reality. This reflects the common conception of language, or the use of linguistic terms, as a supervenient activity which provides a symbolic picture of the real world of facts, physical objects, and things actually happening. For instance, the sentence 'A book is on the table', is believed to symbolise the fact, in the world of reality, that the physical object we call 'a book' is on the physical object we call 'the table'. Thus, it is thought, in order to understand reality man has to conceptualise it in symbols.

The third form of dualism, then, is clearly illustrated in Metheny's distinction between the concept of an event and the event as such. The supposition is that men perceive the real world out there, and form concepts of it in language which mirrors and allows them to comprehend the actual events and objects. Thus the two terms of the dualism are, on the one hand, language and conceptualisation, and, on the other hand, the real world.

The major problem for such a notion is that it implies that all men are inescapably trapped behind what has been aptly called the veil of perception. Concepts are supposed to be necessary in order for men to be able to understand the reality which they perceive, but in that case what justification could there be for supposing there to be a real world, if by that is meant a world which is independent of conception? The point is that no sense can be attached to the notion of a concept-free apprehension of reality. Some philosophers have thought, and it is tempting for the layman to think, that it is intelligible to ask the question: 'What sort of structure ought language to have to mirror reality?' Such a question implies that language could somehow be checked against reality to see whether it provides an accurate picture. But this notion is incoherent, since reality has to be *understood* in order that the supposed check with language can take place. Yet this understanding of reality *itself* can be achieved only *by means of* the conceptualisation given with language. Thus it is a fundamental confusion to regard language or conceptualisation, and reality, as two distinct phenomena.

To put the point another way, it is a consequence of this dualist picture that all men are behind the veil of concepts which give understanding to perception. It is senseless to suggest the possibility of having a look at what is on the other side of the veil, since that perception would obviously have to be conceptualised too. In short, to understand this supposedly real world in order to check the verisimilitude of concepts would require one to have unconceptualised concepts. Small wonder that Wittgenstein (1953) remarked that in philosophy one sometimes reaches the point of feeling constrained to emit inarticulate grunts. Thus, to put the point in terms of this misconceived picture, if there were such a real world, outside the possibility of conceptualisation, then it obviously could be of no possible interest or relevance to us, since its character and existence could not be known. Again, it should be recognised that the impossibility is a logical, not a quasi-empirical, one. For it is not that however hard we try we are unable to reach this supposedly real, unconceptualised world, but that nothing could possibly *count* as reaching it. Thus a paradoxical consequence of this general picture of language and reality is that the supposed world of reality would be unreal since it would be impossible even to discover whether it is there. Consequently there could be no difference between human conception of events and the events themselves, and human conception would simply be *equivalent* to reality and truth.

The foregoing argument should be sufficient to expose the misconception inherent in this common picture of the nature of language, or of the relation between language and the world. However, there is a danger that the rejection of such a notion may give rise to an opposite but equally subjective misconception. As we have seen earlier, it is difficult to deny a thesis without providing a thesis which, while opposed to the former, remains on the same logical level, and thus shares some of its most fundamental misconceptions. Thus in denying that a sunset can be heard one may still give the wrong impression, namely that somehow human auditory powers are not as acute as they might be, or that this is something which cannot be *achieved*. In fact, of course, one wants to move out of this level of explanation altogether by showing that the whole notion of hearing *or* being unable to hear sunsets makes no sense. Similarly, to deny the intelligibility of one side of this dualist picture, namely the supposition of an unconceptualised world of reality, may give the impression that what one means is that only the other side, namely human conceptualisation, is left. And this would imply that the world is what we believe it is, that it is created according to how we decide to form our concepts in language. This is an equally objectionable form of subjectivism, for it carries the consequence that there could be no distinction between belief and truth, since what men believed to be true would actually determine what was true.

What is required is a completely different way of looking at the situation, which will avoid the misleading implications inherent in both the affirmation and the denial of this dualist supposition. The crucial point to recognise is that no sense can be given to the notion that language itself could be true or false. Objectivity is *given* by language, thus although beliefs expressed *within* language can be true or false, it is unintelligible to suppose that *concepts* can be true or false since they are the *standards* of truth or falsity. Perhaps the point can be made clear by means of an example. There is a standard metre in Paris which determines what it is to be a metre. That is, it is solely by reference to this standard, ultimately, that the notion of a metre derives its sense. If there were a doubt about the accuracy of a metre rule it could, in theory, be checked against this standard metre. But no sense could be made of the notion of checking the accuracy of the *standard itself*. Similarly, the concepts implicit in language are the standards by which truth or falsity is determined, hence they determine the *possible* constitution of reality. Consequently, if there were two different societies with different languages and conceptual schemes, no sense could be made of the notion of asking which was the *correct* or *more accurate* one. Such a question would be rather like asking whether the rules of chess were more accurate than the rules of tennis. The movement of a chess piece may or may not be in accordance with the rules, and the belief that it is legitimate may be either true or false, but no sense could be made of asking whether the rules *themselves* were true or false. Such a question is as incoherent as asking whether laws are legal.

It should not be thought, however, that this rules out the possibility of criticism or modification of concepts. Although, as we have seen, it is unintelligible to suppose that a concept can be compared with 'reality', in an *external* sense, it could certainly be criticised *internally*. That is, in terms of the language itself a concept may be shown to be internally inconsistent, or to be incompatible with importantly related concepts, and thus to require revision.

How are we to explain meaning in movement then? It is again illuminating to consider the analogue with linguistic meaning. There is a common misconception that word meanings are the basic building bricks from which the whole structure of the meaning of language is erected. Yet, roughly, the situation is precisely the converse of that. The meaning of a word is given by the various sentences in which it is used, and those sentences derive their meaning from the whole activity of language of which they form an interdependent part. The same is true of the meanings of movements. Meaning requires a context. As we saw in Chapter 5, the meaning of a particular action cannot be explained by a narrow concentration upon the physical movement in isolation. The meaning is given by the *context* of the action, or complex of actions, of which it can be observed to form a part. Precisely the same physical movement may have quite different meanings, i.e. it might be different actions, in different contexts. Although in practice *one* may be obvious, there may be various frames of reference from which the movement can be considered, such as the functional, scientific, aesthetic and moral. For example, a bowler's action in cricket could be considered, respectively, for its effectiveness in dismissing batsmen; as graceful; from a biomechanical point of view; or as unfairly intimidatory.

The range of possibilities of human movement provides a unique variety of experiences, but not because movement is a unique symbol of meaning, or a symbol of unique meaning, or a unique symbol of unique meaning. It is because the feelings which can be experienced while moving cannot be experienced in other ways. This raises another problem for Metheny's supposition of symbolic meaning. For even if it were intelligible, an embarrassing consequence of her own theory is that it contradicts one of her principal aims in proposing it, namely to show that the meaning in movement is unique. If the meaning of a movement were symbolic, in Metheny's sense, that would imply two separate entities—(1) the symbol, (2) what is symbolised—in which case it would be logically possible to use a different symbol for what is symbolised. Thus, so far from movement's having a unique meaning, it would be possible for other physical phenomena to have the *same* meaning by symbolising the same thing. Consequently, in Metheny's terms, a kinestruct or kinecept could not be a unique kinesymbol. On the contrary, a painting could symbolise what the movement symbolises, or, in her terms, could 'conceptualise reality' in the same way.

I submit, then, that the elaborate paraphernalia of symbolic theory obscures rather than clarifies the issue of meaning in movement. We can perceive the meaning of the movement, what sort of movement it is, because we subsume it under a concept which is determined, with some degree of tolerance, by the whole set of circumstances in which it occurs. This is why the meaning and feeling of a movement in a dance are quite different from the meaning and feeling of the same movement from a purely physical point of view, as part of a service action in tennis.

Thus, with certain minor exceptions, and excluding the symbolism which is possible in dance, human movement does not *symbolise* reality, it *is* reality. The experiences it provides are unique, they are not merely vicarious reflections of real-life experiences, through the medium of symbolism.

It is unfortunate that a misconceived polarity has arisen about movement and experience. As a crude characterisation, the movement educationist concentrates on the experience, and regards the observable, quantifiable aspects of movement as relatively unimportant. On the other hand, those of scientific inclination are perfectly happy about the perceivable, quantifiable physical movement, but sometimes tend to be suspicious of talk of the inner experience because it is not observable.

In fact neither aspect, alone, is sufficient. To deny the inner experience is to deny the agent, without whom there would *be* no movement. Yet to deny the observable criteria is equally to deny the experience, since without the criteria the experience could not be identified.

So that perception of human movement is necessary in order to *identify* the meaning of the experience. But without the experience there would be no human movement to perceive.

REFERENCES: CHAPTER 8

Metheny, Eleanor, *Connotations of Movement in Sport and Dance* (Dubuque, Iowa: Wm C. Brown, 1965).

Metheny, Eleanor, *Movement and Meaning* (New York: McGraw-Hill, 1968).

Phenix, P., *Realms of Meaning* (New York: McGraw-Hill, 1964).

Wittgenstein, L., *Philosophical Investigations* (Oxford: Basil Blackwell, 1953).

Chapter 9
Communication in Movement

INTRODUCTION

In this chapter I shall argue that widely held assumptions about non-verbal communication, bodily communication, communication in movement, and the language of movement, are based upon misconceptions which also run through the work of many psychologists, sociologists and anthropologists, as well as much of what is said about communication in the arts. Such a misconception is inherent in the commonly encountered claim within the field of human movement that movement is superior to language as a means of communication. It will be shown that the major source of these confusions is the fundamental misunderstanding of the nature and importance of language which was considered in Chapter 8. In particular, I shall examine Argyle's influential book *Bodily Communication* (1975) since it clearly manifests the major underlying misconception which I want to expose. Indeed, more radically, I shall argue that there is an important sense in which such scientific investigation is not even of the *kind* to account for communication.

LINGUISTIC COMMUNICATION

What seems to underlie the belief that movement communicates more effectively than language is the assumption that every aspect of a person's behaviour reveals, and therefore can be said to communicate, something about him. This belief, often regarded by some of those in the field as almost an article of faith, that *every* movement reveals something about a person, seems a very strange one, and, except in the most banal sense it is difficult to see how it could be justified. However, the principal point which I want to raise is that in this kind of context 'communication' is being used in a sense significantly different from its use to refer to linguistic communication, hence it is unintelligible to compare them. That is, two quite different senses of the term are being conflated by those who talk and write in this way.

One of these senses is most clearly exemplified in, although by no means limited to, the normal verbal exchanges of linguistic communication, hence I shall refer to it as *lingcom* for short. In order for lingcom to take place between you and me it is necessary that I should understand what you say or do in the sense in which you intended it to be understood, and there are criteria by which you can tell whether you have communicated successfully. For instance, if, late at night and just as I was about to retire, you were to say to me 'There's a mouse in your bed', and I were to reply 'Yes, skiing is my favourite sport', then in normal circumstances you would be justified in assuming that I had not understood what you said in the sense in which you intended it, and that therefore you had failed to communicate with me.

Now certainly it is possible to communicate through non-verbal behaviour in a lingcom sense. For example, if you were standing on the opposite side of a swimming pool crowded with noisy bathers, and I wanted to communicate to you, despite my inability to shout above the hubbub, that the water was cold, I could grimace and perform simulated shivering movements. To take other obvious examples, a beckoning gesture, the hitch-hikers' thumbing sign, shaking a fist, and nodding the head, can communicate as effectively as saying in words respectively: 'Come here', 'May I have a lift?', 'I am angry with you', and 'I agree'. In each of these cases, and there are, of course, innumerable others, in order for communication to be accomplished, the movement, or non-verbal behaviour, has to be understood in the sense intended. Nevertheless, although some movements can communicate in a lingcom sense, it is quite obvious that not all or even the great majority of movements do communicate in this sense, in which the crucial distinguishing feature is that the perceiver should understand what was intended to be understood by the performance of the movement concerned.

The confusion to which I want to draw attention is engendered by another use of the term 'communication' which can be most clearly brought out by means of examples. Let us imagine that while waiting outside an examination room I am observed to be fidgeting nervously. It is this sort of case which would tempt some to say, for example, that my fidgeting movements communicate my anxiety about whether I shall be successful in the examination. But it is important to recognise that 'communicate' is being used here in a sense quite different from the lingcom sense, since I certainly did not *intend* my anxiety to be noticed, or my movements to be understood in any way at all. On the contrary, I may well have been trying to give the impression of calm confidence. Consider another example. During a prolonged and tedious committee meeting I am eventually unable to stifle an embarrassingly obvious yawn. Those who use the term in the sense we are now considering would say that the yawn communicates my boredom, but clearly this, too, is not a case of lingcom since I certainly did not intend my boredom to be recognised.

This lack of the requisite intention may seem unimportant, yet it is precisely because it is overlooked that the confusions about the notion of communication arise. To appreciate why this is so, let us consider what this latter sense of the term amounts to. According to such a usage my behaviour communicates something to you merely by your perceiving that it is a sign or indication of something about me without, on my part, any intention that my behaviour should be understood in this or any sense. Since communication in this sense is effected simply by the perception of some feature which is taken to be a sign of something else, I shall refer to it as *percom*. This characterisation reveals not only the significance of the difference between such a usage and lingcom, but also that it can equally legitimately be applied to inanimate phenomena. For example, it would have to be agreed that since the rustling of leaves is a sign that the wind is blowing, the leaves communicate; since an unpleasant smell is a sign that the milk has turned sour, the smell communicates; since a snowdrop is a sign of spring, the snowdrop communicates. In short, any feature, whether of animate or inanimate phenomena, which can be perceived by any of the senses to be an indication or evidence of something can be said, in this sense of the term, to communicate.

To emphasise the distinction between the two senses, it may be illuminating to show what would be required to change the examples of percom given above into cases of lingcom. Imagine that while I am waiting outside the examination room I catch your eye and quite deliberately simulate nervous, fidgeting movements. Now I *do* intend you to notice them and to understand them as meaning that I am worried about the examination. Similarly, in the committee meeting I might catch the eye of a colleague and surreptitiously perform a simulated yawn. He knows very well that this is not a genuine yawn, and recognises that my actions are performed with the intention that he should understand that I am bored. Such cases are quite different from the original example in which there was no intention that the nervous behaviour and yawn, respectively, should be understood in any sense at all, or even noticed.

The similar ambiguity in the use of the term 'meaning' may partly explain how 'communication' came to be used in the percom sense. For instance, it may already be significant of his conflation of the two senses, and his consequent confusion in the concept of communication, that Argyle writes: 'Signals are a quite distinctive class of behaviour, because they have meanings.' But not every case in which we speak of meaning is a case where it would make sense to speak of communication; for example: 'Excessive oil consumption means a worn engine.' Obviously there can be no intention to be understood here, and it is an indication of a barbarous misuse that in the percom sense it would be equally legitimate to say that the excessive oil consumption *communicates* that the engine is worn. In such a case 'A means B' is roughly equivalent to 'A is a sign or evidence of B'. Yet this is parallel to the percom sense of communication. In this use of 'meaning' one could say, for instance, 'The rustling of the leaves means that the wind is blowing'; and 'That smell means that the milk has turned sour'. In these cases, too, it would sound very odd if one were to substitute 'communicates' for 'means'.

Some of those who use the term in the percom sense, on hearing my argument, have expressed uneasiness about this consequence. But if 'communicates' is to be used so widely that it is equivalent to 'is a sign of', and where there is no intention to be understood, then there is no justification for excluding its application to inanimate objects. Argyle appears not to recognise this consequence of such a usage, since in his investigations into bodily *communication* he considers pupillary dilation, dimensions of physique, and even the recognition of identity. Yet it is significant of precisely this consequence that, in normal circumstances when someone recognises you walking along a road, it would sound very odd to say that you have *communicated* your identity. Indeed, if the term be extended so far that even recognising the identity of someone or something can be regarded as a case of communication, then there is a danger of its becoming completely vacuous, since in that case, presumably, everything that can be known is communicated. One encounters other examples in the literature and in discussion on human movement of the use of the term in a similarly degenerate way, such that statements made about communication in movement become devoid of content.

Wittgenstein (1967) brings out the point in this way:

> 'The dog *means* something by wagging his tail'—What grounds would one give for saying this?—Does one also say: 'By drooping its leaves, the plant means that it needs water'? We should hardly ask if the crocodile means something when it comes at a man with open jaws. And we should declare that since the crocodile cannot think there is really no question of meaning here.

As I suggested above, the ambiguity in the meaning of 'meaning' may explain to some extent how it is that the meaning of 'communication' has become extended in such a way that it cannot legitimately be restricted to animate creatures. For in one sense of 'meaning' it is perfectly legitimate to substitute 'communication' or a cognate expression. For example, instead of saying 'My simulated yawn means that I am bored', one could use the synonymous expression 'My yawn communicates that I am bored'. Then perhaps the ambiguity in 'means' is overlooked, and the meaning of 'communicates' slides degenerately into the former term's other sense. The point can be illustrated by reference to the quotation given above. It makes perfectly good sense to say 'Its drooping leaves mean (i.e. are a sign) that the plant needs water', whereas it would be absurd to suggest that therefore by drooping its leaves the plant means or communicates that it needs water.

Although they are unable to justify it, the uneasy feeling of those who use the term in the percom sense that it should somehow be restricted solely to animate creatures may provide a clue to another source of the slide in the meaning of 'communication'. For what almost certainly underlies this feeling is the notion that 'communication', when properly used, is somehow importantly related to intentions, and only animate creatures are capable of intentions. In that case there is something substantially correct in this vague feeling, as will be clear from the account I have given so far. Yet, in the case of animate creatures it is very easy to overlook the important distinction to which I have drawn attention, since gestures, facial expressions, and other bodily actions may be intentional without being cases of lingcom, or, as I should now prefer to put it, genuine cases of communication. For it should be emphasised that the intention required for lingcom is not just a simple one. The action must be not merely intentional but performed with the intention of producing the requisite belief in the observer by means of his recognition of that intention. Thus it might be said that in order to communicate, an action necessarily requires a double intention, in that it has to be not only simply intended, but *also* intended in the more complex sense that the intention with which it is performed be recognised. To put the point in a simpler, if circular, way, in order for communication to be effected the perceiver has to recognise not just an intended action, but an action intended to communicate by means of a recognition of the intention to communicate. Thus, when I am walking to the shops my actions are intentional in the simple sense, and I intend to walk to the shops. But I certainly do not intend anything to be understood by such actions. This reveals how mistaken it is to suppose that even all *intentional* actions, or actions performed with an intention, can legitimately be said to communicate, since it is quite clear that the great majority of such actions, gestures and facial expressions are performed without any intention that they should be understood in some way by anyone else. Consequently, it is a confusion to suggest that *all* movements communicate, or constitute a language, or to compare movement or action with language with respect to effectiveness of communication.

It may be true that 'communication' in the degenerate percom sense applies to all movement, since this amounts merely to the claim that all movement is a sign of something or other. (Indeed, as we have seen, in the percom sense 'communication' is in danger of degenerating to complete vacuity.) But this is quite different from the obviously false claim that all movement communicates in a lingcom sense. Yet in discussion of human movement the confusing nature of the common claim that all movement communicates is largely unrecognised because of an elision of the two senses. In short:

(1) 'All movement communicates' (percom) may be true in the somewhat trivial sense that all movement is an indication of something or other, just as any sound or smell is an indication of something or other.

(2) 'All movement communicates' (lingcom) is a much more substantial claim, but it is patently false.

I said above that the argument reveals the advisability of referring to the relevant cases not as lingcom but as genuine cases of communication. For, as I hope is now clear, the term 'percom' was introduced solely as a heuristic device, in order to expose the confusion which emanates from the slide in the meaning of 'communication'. No doubt there will be those who will object that it is arbitrary to insist that the term should be restricted to cases of the kind which I have characterised as lingcom since, they may say, I am merely stipulating how it should be used. Perhaps I can refer anyone inclined to such a view to the precisely similar objection considered in Chapter 7 with respect to 'art'. Although of course the meaning of a word may change, and one may decide to use a word in a special sense, as in a code, I have tried to show that there are good reasons for continuing to insist on this restriction on the use of 'communication'. A change in its use will not remove, although as we have seen from the consequent confusions, it is likely to blur, the distinction to which I have drawn attention. In short, some stipulations about the way words should be used are far from being merely arbitrary, since other uses may lead to serious misconception.

It may be worth briefly mentioning the relationship of communication to conventional or standard meaning. It would be implausible to suggest that a verbal term has meaning only when it is being used with the intention to communicate. On the contrary, it is obvious that the meaning of a word is not lost even if there are no tokens of it actually in use at any particular time. Moreover, there is clearly a distinction between the standard meaning of a verbal term, and what it may be used to mean, for example in a code. It would be too much of a diversion to consider standard meaning in the detail it requires, but it is worth pointing out that the intention to communicate, as I have characterised it, provides the basis for an account of such meaning. Roughly, such an account would follow these lines: a mark or sound is used by individual people with the intention to communicate, i.e. with lingcom intention, and progressively within a society it comes to be generally used in this way, and in due course becomes ossified into a convention. Thus its use to produce the requisite belief becomes standardised. However, the change from general to standard use is complex. It should certainly not be assumed that they are equivalent. 'Disinterested' is commonly, perhaps generally, used as synonymous with 'uninterested', but that is not what it means. The change from general usage to standard meaning will have been accomplished only when it makes sense to say that the sound or mark is being used correctly or incorrectly. That is, it is the standard meaning which determines what is to count as correct usage. And only when a sound or mark has reached this point can it intelligibly be regarded as a word or term in a language. The same applies, of course, to non-verbal behaviour which generates standard meaning.

However, although this is an important issue and obviously closely related to the theme of this chapter, it should be understood that a discussion of standard meaning in language *is* a diversion from the topic of *communication*. I mention the point because the objection has been made against my account that I put all the emphasis on intentions and do not allow for syntax, truth conditions, and conventions, all of which, it was argued, are necessary for an adequate account of the communication of meaning in language. But this objection is confused. It is true that such factors would be required for an adequate account of standard meaning in language, although even here I would argue that the complex intentions I have characterised in lingcom are *primary*, in that these other factors develop *as a consequence*, and in the way I have outlined. Thus I would argue that even if I were giving an account of standard meaning I should be justified in placing greater emphasis on intention than on these other factors. But more importantly, my concern is *not* with standard meaning, whether in verbal or non-verbal language, but with *communication*. And where communication is concerned, whether by the use of standard meanings or not, then it is achieved *solely* by means of the recognition of an intention to produce in the hearer or observer the requisite belief. To see this, consider a case where, purely fortuitously, cracks appear in a brick wall in the form of a word with standard meaning. Obviously a wall cannot communicate. On the other hand, the cracks could have been created in order to communicate. In that case successful communication would consist in the recognition by an observer of the intention to produce the requisite belief by the use of those cracks.

A further point which should be recognised is that communication is not always and necessarily completely successful, but is often a matter of degree of understanding of the relevant intention. For instance, teachers at all levels are often faced with problems created by a range of degrees of comprehension in student audiences. Up to a point one would want to say that there had been some communication, but beyond that point it would have to be conceded that no communication had effectively been accomplished. This issue becomes more complicated in relation to communication in the arts, as we shall see.

Before leaving this part of the argument let me emphasise again that lingcom is not limited to *verbal* exchanges, but is the kind of communication most clearly exemplified in verbal language. Moreover, I certainly do not deny, indeed I would insist, that gestures, facial expressions, and so on may contribute to verbal communication in such a way that they cannot coherently be distinguished from it. There is a common misconception that language necessarily involves *words*, and is thus distinct from behaviour. Yet it is important to recognise that language itself is a *form* of behaviour, and a principal aim of this chapter is to show *what* distinguishes it from non-linguistic behaviour. That is, no line can usefully, or even coherently, be drawn between communication which employs words and that which does not. The crucial distinction is between non-intentional and intentional behaviour of the kind described above. The point becomes clear when one considers people who have language but not words in the normal sense, as in deaf-and-dumb language. This is one reason why many philosophers regard the sentence, and not the word, as the basic unit of language, since, for instance, to say 'Door' and point may be the equivalent of 'Would you please close the door', or of 'Would you please leave'. Simply pointing, without saying anything, may be enough. Similarly, placing a finger to one's lips is equivalent in some contexts to saying 'Please be as quiet as possible'. These examples clearly reveal that the only coherent way to characterise language is not by reference to the employment of words, but as a form of intentional behaviour which may employ words, but which certainly need not do so. In short, contrary to the prevalent misconception, it is a mistake to assume that 'linguistic' is equivalent to 'verbal'. Argyle seems to fail to recognise this point, with damaging consequences.

Nevertheless, although it is oblique to the main theme of this chapter, it may be worth pointing out that some people in the field of human movement seem much too ready to denigrate the usefulness of words. For instance, it is often assumed that movement is a universal language which communicates better than words. Such an assumption is presumably implicit in Valerie Preston's (1963) statement that 'movement is such a vast language, far bigger than the language of words'. And Bruce and Tooke (1966) write: 'Movement is a language which the ordinary person may use more easily than any other to express those feelings, ideas and experiences which transcend words.' But consider the difficulty of expressing the argument of this book solely in physical movement. Indeed, those who argue for the supremacy of movement as a means of communication put themselves in an ironically self-defeating position, since it is worth noting that they themselves employ the resources of *verbal* language in order to propound their case.

However, what I wish to emphasise is the much more important point that a language is not merely a system of signs to convey messages. The commonly assumed equivalence of 'linguistic' and 'verbal' seems to contribute to or reflect this misapprehension. Yet, as we saw in Chapter 8, it is fundamentally misconceived to regard language as a mere convenience, supervenient to the activities and behaviour of people. On the contrary, language provides the standards of truth and falsity; it gives the structure of possible reality, as the expression of the whole form of life of a society.

COMMUNICATION IN DANCE

For communication in dance and the arts generally the transmission and recognition of the relevant intention is still necessary, although the point is often overlooked. For example, Horst (1969) writes, 'the moment we speak of emotion communication is involved. If you get excited about a dancer even without knowing it, she is communicating to you.' It is clear that the term is being used in the percom sense here, hence the odd conclusion, for, to take an obvious counter-example, someone watching a tragic dance might become erotically excited by the dancer. Such an inappropriate response would count to that extent *against* effective communication of what is being expressed in the dance.

I hope by now it is clear that I certainly do not wish to imply that communication can occur only by means of movements which can be translated into words, although the simple examples given at the beginning of the chapter may initially have conveyed that impression. On the contrary, the notion of communication in dance and the other arts is greatly complicated by the impossibility of identifying artistic meaning apart from its particular medium of expression. This raises problems which cannot be adequately considered here, although I have discussed them more fully elsewhere (1974). However, it is necessary to consider those aspects of the issue which are concerned with communication. We saw in Chapter 7 that the purpose of a work of art cannot be comprehensively characterised in any way other than the work itself, and precisely the same point applies to its meaning. What is expressed in a dance, for example, cannot be comprehensively expressed in words, music or painting. The only complete description of its meaning is given by the dance itself, thus the meaning is uniquely related to those particular forms of physical movement. For example, a celebrated Russian dancer, asked what was the meaning of one of her dances, replied with exasperation: 'If I could say it in so many words, do you think I should take the very great trouble of dancing it?'

This poses two related problems for communication in dance and the other arts: (1) How can it be known that communication has been effected?; and (2) Does the logical requirement of the recognition of the relevant intention imply that communication is possible only where there is definitive artistic meaning?

(1) With respect to the former problem, it might seem to follow from the fact that artistic meaning and medium of expression cannot coherently be regarded as logically distinct that spectators after a dance performance could not reveal their comprehension of it in discussion. Yet clearly this is the principal way in which someone's capacity for sensitive artistic appreciation is judged. The words he uses at the time may be unable to give the whole picture, but they can provide a fairly clear outline. We can, as it were, continue to follow the verbal lines of direction beyond the point at which the words come to an end. However, there is a danger that this way of putting it will lead to a misunderstanding, for it is not in the least to concede that there is a residue of some sort of subjective comprehension which could not be characterised by reference to overt behaviour. It is to make the point that in the sphere of the arts the notion of understanding can be very complex. To determine whether someone has fully understood and appreciated a dance performance it may be necessary implicitly to take into account much wider factors than what he says at any one time. It may require an implicit reference to the whole background of his behaviour with respect not only to dance but also to other arts and indeed to related non-artistic aspects of life. For example, what he has said about other dance performances and other works of art, the kinds of performances he attends and works of art in which he is interested, the enthusiasm he evinces for relevantly similar works and performances, and the nature and sensitivity of his understanding of people in life generally, are the kinds of factors which may all contribute to justifying our judgement that what he says and does *now* manifests a comprehensive understanding of *this* dance performance. To give a simple analogue, one could not assume that the utterance of a sentence or mathematical formula necessarily revealed

an understanding of language or mathematics, since a parrot could be taught to utter either. It will be recalled from Chapter 5 that it is a mistake to believe that the character of an action must be identifiable solely by what can be discerned to happen at the time of its occurrence. Similarly, to assume *either* that it must be possible to reveal a complete understanding of a work of art or artistic performance by what one says or does *at the time, or* that otherwise there must be some subjective residue, is to manifest a fundamental misconception about the nature of thought and understanding *in general*. For this situation is by no means limited to the arts. To be able to judge someone's thought about and understanding of many other aspects of life, such as the understanding of people, equally requires an implicit reference to far wider factors than what can be said at any *one* time.

Moreover, there are various non-verbal ways of revealing artistic understanding at the time. Rapt attention, laughter, facial expressions, and so on during a performance, and one's mood afterwards, perhaps of exhilaration or contemplative melancholy, can often provide clear indications of understanding.

(2) As we have seen, communication is not always a case of all-or-nothing, but rather a matter of degree. This is especially true of the arts where the notion of communication is enormously complicated by the variety of possible interpretations. For there is generally a far greater degree of tolerance in what could count as correct artistic meaning, than in correct linguistic meaning. In contrast to a work of art, the possibility of various interpretations of a linguistic statement is generally a fault. For instance, where a dance is so complex that it cannot be described simply, even in a broad, undiscriminating way, there is likely to be a commensurately large number of subtly varied responses and interpretations, each of which, from perceptive and knowledgeable spectators, may be regarded as correct. Thus no sense could be given to the notion of 'the definitive' meaning of the work. Nevertheless, in order for communication to be effected there must be some degree of correspondence between the intentions of the dancer or choreographer and the response of the spectator, even though the correspondence may not be complete. That is, the spectator must be able to understand to some extent the intention of the artist, which is expressed in and logically inseparable from the particular medium of expression.

In this respect it is important to avoid a very common but seriously damaging misconception arising from the possibility of a range of equally valid interpretations of a work of art. For this certainly should not be taken to imply that there are *no* limits where artistic meaning is concerned, since that notion would involve the incoherent subjectivism, and therefore the impossibility of any meaning, which we

Communication in Movement/149

considered in Chapter 8. Perceptive critics have argued for various interpretations of Shakespeare's *King Lear*, but anyone who saw the play as a comedy would obviously be wrong, since this would have transgressed the boundaries of intelligible interpretation. The crucial point to understand is that although the possibility of correct or intelligible interpretation of a work of art may be indefinite, it certainly cannot be unlimited. Different cultural traditions may set different limits to the area within which interpretations could be understood as correct, and even within the same society there may be different schools and styles. The conventions, and with them the limits of correct interpretation, are always open to modification and extension. Someone whose experience of dance has been exclusively or predominantly within the tradition of classical ballet may find it difficult to understand the work of Martha Graham, Paul Taylor or Alwin Nikolais. And experience solely of Western conventions will allow only a shallow comprehension, at most, of oriental dance. Without some knowledge of the artistic tradition it would be impossible adequately to understand an artist's work, and thus the degree of communication, if any, would be negligible. In this way artistic meaning and appreciation are tied to socio-historical context. Clearly this raises insuperable problems for those who, like Bruce (1965), make the commonly encountered assertion that dance is a universal language. For in fact it is no more possible for dance than it is for a verbal language to be universally understood, at least at anything above a very primitive level. It is strange that this sort of claim is often made by those whose central concern is with dance in education, since the consequences, if they were right, would be so damaging to their own position. However, I hope that enough has been said to show that the claim that dance is a universal language, quite apart from the inherent misconception involved, does dance, and especially dance in education, a grave disservice. For there is much to *learn* if one is to understand dance or any other art form.

Individual differences of sensitivity and natural aptitude also inevitably affect the possibility of understanding the arts. The unperceptive may be able to achieve only a crude, general idea of the meaning of a dance performance, since fully to appreciate the arts requires the capacity imaginatively to grasp and respond to complex interpretations. Clearly these considerations also affect the degree of communication which is possible between dancer or choreographer and spectator.

Before leaving this topic it is worth pointing out that the argument exposes as a myth the prevalent notion that great art should be readily comprehensible by all mankind. There is just as much to *learn*, fully to understand a deep and complex work of art, as a scientific theory. On this point I have sometimes fallen foul of some Marxists who have objected that it implies an élitist attitude to the arts. This seems a strange objection since they do not apply the same political and moral criteria to 'élitism' in the sciences. I cannot see that my argument has any political implications at all. As Shahn (1957) puts it:

> It is not the degree of communicability that constitutes the value of art to the public. It is its basic intent and responsibility. A work of art in which powerful passion is innate, or which contains extraordinary revelations concerning form, or manifests brilliant thinking, however difficult its language, will serve ultimately to dignify that society in which it exists. By the same argument, a work that is tawdry and calculating in intent is not made more worthy by being easily understood. One does not judge an Einstein equation by its communicability, but by its actual content and meaning.

SYMBOLIC MEANING AGAIN

Consideration of the topic of communication, and especially empirical work on the subject, is frequently vitiated by the underlying misconceptions about meaning and mental concepts which have been examined in earlier chapters. Argyle's widely influential book *Bodily Communication* (1975) is a good example of sophisticated empirical research which can be shown clearly to exhibit the deep conceptual errors to which I want to draw attention. However, it should be emphasised that the criticisms which I shall make do not denigrate the importance of scientific investigation into, for example, personality traits, as long as it is carried out in the appropriate spheres. One can, of course, learn a great deal about a person by observing those aspects of his behaviour which are not intended to communicate in any sense. And the kind of research undertaken by Argyle will no doubt increase our knowledge. I do not in the least wish to be taken as denying that a person's movements, way of talking, walking, and so on may contradict and be more revealing than what he says. This, presumably, is what some of the authors are getting at who make extravagant claims about human movement. However, it should be remembered that the converse may also be true, in that one's judgement of a person on the basis of his non-verbal behaviour may be *corrected* by what he says. But more importantly, it is a profound misconception to overlook the crucial distinction in *kind* between behaviour which does, and behaviour which does not, involve the complex intention I have characterised as lingcom. For to do so leads to confusions which are manifest in statements which imply, or even openly state, that movement is superior to or transcends language as a means of communication. The implied comparison is as incoherent as supposing that sight transcends hearing, on the grounds that it is impossible to hear the colours of a sunset. More importantly, this whole oversimple conception of language overlooks the vast and heterogeneous range of feelings, ideas and experiences which are given *solely* by language. For instance, creatures without language may be able to move, but it would be unintelligible to suggest that they could hope for or fear what may occur in a year's time, since nothing could amount to their experiencing such feelings.

Perhaps the most damaging misconception running through Argyle's work is one which we considered in Chapter 8, namely that of regarding the meaning of words or actions as what they symbolise or stand for. Since Argyle shares this common assumption, he is almost inevitably led to an unfortunate conception of language as a code in which those meanings can be communicated. He writes: 'Communication of all kinds can be looked at in terms of a sender who encodes and a receiver who decodes, so that a signal has a meaning for each of them', and: 'In discussions of communication it is usually supposed that there is an encoder, a message, and a decoder.' But although such a conception is plausible, it is seriously misleading. For the notion of a code presupposes and therefore cannot be equivalent to a language, since it is intelligible only in terms of a language. That is, it is always possible to identify any encoded message independently of the code in which it is conveyed. Thus to regard language itself as a code implies that what is expressed in language is independent of language. I think Argyle would be happy to accept this consequence, since he writes of a *correlation* between language and thought, and when A is correlated with B, then A and B are independently identifiable. For example, it makes sense to say that there is a correlation between smoking and lung cancer because smoking and lung cancer can be independently identified.

Now certainly a proposition or thought may be logically independent of any *particular* formulation in language, since there are synonymous expressions, and propositions can be translated into other languages, but it cannot intelligibly be supposed that a proposition could be independent of *any* linguistic formulation whatsoever. For this would incur the untenable consequence, revealed in Chapter 8 with respect to concepts, that no sense could be given to the notions of understanding, language, and therefore of communication. Nothing could amount to a correlation between the inner meaning or thought which you encode into a sentence, and the inner meaning or thought into which I decode it. On the hypothesis that ideas or thoughts are extra-linguistic mental events or entities which are encoded into and decoded from linguistic terms, it would be intelligible to suppose a mouse to be capable of fear of economic inflation, although not yet able to use the code in which to express it. Similarly, it would make sense to suggest that a parrot may mean the words it utters since it may be encoding the appropriate private mental ideas. Conversely, since it is supposed that a listener decodes the verbal expression by translating it into his own mental idea, nothing could amount to knowing into which ideas, if any, sentences were being decoded. Consequently, as nothing can count as checking the ideas supposedly being encoded and decoded in the case of every other person, the conception of language as a code for the transmission of language-independent messages collapses into incoherence.

Argyle is similarly confused about other mental concepts, again as a consequence of this erroneous theory of meaning. Thus he says: 'some non-verbal signals stand for emotions'. But, for instance, anger-behaviour cannot merely *stand for* and therefore be contingently, i.e. non-logically, related to anger, since this notion would incur the incoherent consequence that any sort of behaviour could express any sort of emotion or none. For on this hypothesis the only way to discover for which emotion certain behaviour stands would be actually to *experience* the inner emotion of another person. And since, in this sense, nothing could possibly amount to experiencing someone else's emotions, no sense could be made even of the supposition that other people *do* have emotions. It will not help, of course, to suggest that the problem can be overcome by supposing that other people experience what I do when I behave in a similar way. For again, the only way in which such a supposition could be justified would be actually to experience their emotions. Thus there could be no way of knowing whether behaviour which for me is an expression of extreme anxiety is for other people an expression of great joy, or even of no emotion at all. In the same vein, Argyle writes of verbal 'labels' for emotions. But again, on such a view, it would make sense to suppose that a mouse could have fear of inflation but, as it happens, he has not yet learned the correct label for this feeling. Yet, as we saw in Chapter 8, *only* the ability to use the relevant linguistic expressions could possibly count as having such a feeling. Thus the notion that the behaviour or emotion word stands for, or is a sign of, or label for, and therefore merely correlated with, the relevant feeling, also collapses into incoherence. (This is not, of course, to deny that it is a contingent matter that certain marks or sounds rather than others are used to refer to certain emotions.) No sense can be made of any theory which proposes that the behaviour or linguistic term merely stands for, or is a label of, an emotion, and certainly such a view would preclude the *communication*, in any sense of that term, of emotions. The behaviour or linguistic term can coherently be regarded only as *logically* related to the emotion, in that, to put it roughly, it would make no sense to suppose, *in general*, that this kind of behaviour did not express this kind of emotion. And in learning the language one learns *what* kind.

The clearest example of this misconception is revealed in Argyle's account of the non-verbal arts. He writes: 'It looks as if what is being expressed in music is an elaborate sequence of inner experiences including various emotions. It is because music can represent these experiences so well that it has been called "the language of the emotions"'. But it is difficult to know what could be meant by asserting that music *represents* emotions, and it is unintelligible to suppose that there could be an 'elaborate sequence of inner experiences' existing independently in the mind, and which are as a matter of contingent fact expressed in music. For how can their existence be verified? Apart from the possibility of their expression in music how could they be identified? It is significant that Argyle writes of music that it can represent these experiences '*so well*'. This suggests that various methods of representation have been or could be tried, and, as a matter of empirical fact, it has been discovered that music is the most effective. But this whole conception is incoherent, for it is *only* their possible expression in music which identifies such emotions or experiences. Thus without such possible expression they could not even be intelligibly supposed to exist. Certainly no sense could be made of the suggestion that perhaps the *same* emotions could be expressed in some other way, even if not so well. For nothing else could possibly count as the same emotion. That is, the relation between the 'inner experience' and the overt musical expression is a logical one. This, of course, is an aspect of the issue we discussed in Chapter 6, concerning the incoherence of the notion of the experience *itself*, in isolation from external criteria, constituted in this case by music. Argyle also says that music is *one means* of expressing emotions and attitudes which could not be adequately put into words. This again implies or suggests that there is no impossibility in principle, but only in practice, about expressing these emotions in some other form. But it is not just a *practical* impossibility which prevents the sadness of Mozart's Fortieth Symphony from being expressed in some other way. The impossibility is logical. It does not make sense to suppose that it could be expressed in any other way. It may be recalled that in Chapter 8 we considered the fundamental misconception inherent in Eleanor Metheny's statement that the meanings the mover expresses and the meanings understood by the observer are *probably* never identical. Argyle's statement that music can represent the relevant inner experiences *so well* is a manifestation of precisely the same misconception. In both cases it is supposed that the inner experiences or meanings can intelligibly be said to exist independently of any form of expression. And both authors fail to recognise the nature of the consequent difficulty of explaining what could count as the expression of such inner experiences. Argyle, too, clearly conceives of it on the model of an empirical problem, whereas it is as logically impossible for these experiences to be expressed in another way as to construct a four-sided triangle. That is, just as nothing could amount to a four-sided triangle, so nothing could amount to the expression of *the same* experiences in another way. For example, what sense could be made of the supposition that in fact a painter had at last succeeded in constructing a painting which was another means of expressing the sadness of Mozart's Fortieth Symphony, even if not quite so well? It certainly would not be necessary to go and inspect the painting to discover whether the claim were justified, any more than inspection would be required to discover whether it were true that someone had constructed a four-sided triangle. On Argyle's model it would have to be intelligible to suppose that a poem or painting could be found to express an inner experience *even better*, so that the music became redundant. That is, on this view, it would make sense to say: 'There is no need to bother to go to the concert. Stay at home and read this poem which expresses the same emotions even better than the music.'

Argyle clearly regards it as intelligible to suppose that the inner experiences exist prior to and independently of any form of expression. But in that case, how could they be identified, and how could they be known to exist? The point could be brought home forcibly to anyone of this persuasion if we were to ask to *which* experiences he is referring. For the *only* way in which that question can be answered is by reference to the relevant piece of music. The point is precisely the same as that raised in Chapter 6 with respect to the experience of the performer. If he identifies the experience by saying, as he moves 'It feels like *this*' he concedes the point I am making. For there is no way of identifying the 'it' (the experience) *apart from* the 'this' (the observable behaviour). Analogously, the relevant emotions and experiences are uniquely identified by, and thus cannot coherently be supposed to exist independently of, their overt musical forms of expression.

REASONS AND CAUSES AGAIN

A related misconception which runs through Argyle's book, and which, as we saw in Chapter 5, is one to which those engaged in empirical inquiry are prone, arises from his failure to distinguish between reasons and causes, and thus his tendency to assume that all explanation is of a causal nature. For instance, he seems to believe that the meaning of a work of art is to be discovered by investigating causal responses to it. Thus he writes, with respect to the *meaning* of music, that some people raise their heads or contract certain muscles when the music rises, and that there are physiological reactions, such as an increase in heart-rate when one listens to loud and exciting music. But as we have seen in Chapter 5, explanations of causal effects are quite different from explanations of meaning, whether artistic or linguistic. To give a physiological account of human reactions to musical sound is nothing like giving an account of the meaning of the music. Similarly, questions of the causal effects of background music on increased productivity of factory workers are quite different from questions of its meaning.

In order to make the point quite clear let me approach the issue from another direction. Let us suppose that a psychologist, anthropologist or sociologist carries out an investigation of a completely alien group of creatures. After a time he discovers well-established correlations between the occurrence of certain sounds they utter and the reactions of those who hear the sounds. He is now in a position accurately to predict the reactions of the creatures to the relevant sounds. But has he *ipso facto* discovered that they have a language, or discovered something about the meaning of the language, and therefore about the communication which occurs between them? Clearly not, or, at least, not necessarily, any more than discovering the causal effects of a chess move would be the same as discovering the meaning in terms of the game. It may be worth repeating the quotation from Wittgenstein (1953) already cited in Chapter 5:

When I say that the orders 'Bring me sugar' and 'Bring me milk' make sense, but not the combination 'Milk me sugar', that does not mean that the utterance of this combination of words has no effect. And if its effect is that the other person stares at me and gapes, I don't on that account call it the order to stare and gape, even if that was precisely the effect that I wanted to produce.

Even if the utterance of that combination were found regularly and generally to produce that causal effect, such a correlation could not answer the question of whether it has meaning or sense. Similarly, referring back to the empirical investigation of the alien creatures, my point is that to establish whether there is communication or language will require the development of some understanding of the point or meaning of what is being uttered or done. And that is a totally different sort of enterprise from discovering the causal effects of what is being uttered or done. It is a failure to recognise this important distinction which leads some to assume far too easily that there is language or communication between animals. (Anthropomorphism, often unrecognised, also contributes largely to misconceptions on this topic.)

As we have seen, a word, in isolation from a language, is not a word but merely a meaningless sound. It can be a word only when used as an interdependent part of a language according to certain implicit rules. Hence no purely *external* investigation, conducted from outside the institution of its possible use, could settle the question of whether a sound has any meaning. Consequently, no such external investigation could answer questions of communication generally. By contrast, it would, of course, be possible to conduct an external investigation into causal effects of utterances and behaviour.

Of course this is not to deny that empirical analysis of the causal effects of social interaction may be valuable. My point is that, contrary to what is commonly believed by those inclined towards the assumption that all human action is in principle scientifically explicable, it is not merely that human social interaction involves a much more *complex* set of causal responses than does the interaction of animals, although that may be true, but that, far more importantly, there is a crucial difference of *kind* involved here. That difference consists in the fact that human beings have language, which gives rationality, the possibility of ascribing intentions, and therefore, as will be clear from the earlier characterisation of lingcom, the possibility of communication. (For a discussion of the relation between language and rationality see Bennett, 1964.) This again emphasises how serious an underestimation it is of the significance of language to conceive it as merely a code or message-carrying activity. On the contrary, a language is an expression of a conception of reality, and it is only from within that conception that any intention and therefore action of a member of that linguistic community can be characterised. Consequently, it makes no sense to suppose that an external, causal, stimulus-response kind of explanation could account for communication. An examination of communication has to be *internal* to a language, it has to *presuppose* understanding, hence it is quite different in kind from an investigation of causal connections.

The point can be brought out by reference again to the chess example adduced in Chapter 5. The intention of a player cannot be characterised externally, i.e. independently of the rules and conventions of the game. To see this, imagine a scientifically trained observer, with no knowledge of chess or any relevantly similar game, attempting to characterise in terms external to the game the intention of a player in making a move. He would have to give an account in terms of something like the apparently aimless moving of an oddly carved little piece of wood on a black and white patterned board. But clearly this would not be an adequate account of the player's intention. His intention is not simply to move a piece of wood, but to use his bishop to checkmate his opponent. Outside the conventions of chess this intention cannot be formulated or understood.

There is an objection which could be raised against me by a behaviouristically inclined scientist. He may accept my main point that any legitimate account of communication necessarily involves the attribution of intentions, but he may deny that it is impossible to account for this in causal or external scientific terms. On the contrary, he may claim, although it has not yet in fact been achieved, it is in principle possible to discover the character of intentions by scientific investigation. It might, for instance, be discovered scientifically that whenever people have a particular intention I, it is found to correlate with a specific brain-state B. Thus, he may claim, it could be discovered that there is an identity relation between I and B, or, in short, that the brain-state just *is* the intention, and this could be discovered scientifically and externally.

Well, let us consider precisely what this contention amounts to. If the objector is claiming that I and B are *logically* equivalent, in that it would make as little sense to suppose that one could recognise the intention without recognising the brain-state as to suppose that one could recognise a bachelor without recognising an unmarried man, then the objection is easily refuted. For it is obviously possible to recognise the character of intentional actions without any knowledge of brain-states. Indeed, intentions could be ascribed even by people who were unaware that animate beings have brains. Hence it cannot be true that recognising an intention is logically equivalent to recognising a brain-state.

However, there is a more plausible and sophisticated version of this objection which is often proposed. It is said that the identity relation between I and B is not logical but contingent. That is, there is a brain-state B which is identical in the sense of having a one-to-one correlation with intention I, and it is possible in principle that this will be discovered in due course by scientific investigation. It is important to grasp the difference between this and the previous version. According to the former, it is as logically impossible for anything to be an intention which is not a brain-state as it is for anything to be a bachelor which is not an unmarried man. There is obviously no correlation here. But in the version we are now considering, the claim is that as a matter of contingent fact I always goes with B, and this is in principle empirically discoverable. This is to claim, against my argument, that an intentional action *can* be characterised *externally*, namely by reference to a brain-state. For example, it would be claimed, against me, that such an external account could be given of the intentional action of the chess player, i.e. it does not necessarily require an implicit reference to the rules and conventions of the game. On this view the character of the intention would be given in some such way as: 'What I see is a case of intentional action I, i.e. that which is invariably caused by brain-state B.'

This sort of argument is often adduced, and it is a tempting line of thought for those of scientific inclination. However, although I have done my best to present it as clearly as possible, it seems to me inherently obscure. Its plausibility derives from the peculiar logical status of the claim to contingent *identity*, which appears surreptitiously to trade on the former version of the identity thesis we have just discussed. That is, the term 'contingent identity' is almost self-contradictory, since 'identity' normally carries implications of *logical* equivalence. Thus it is clearer to avoid the term and discuss the claim in terms of a *correlation* of intention with brain-state. It should be noticed that in these terms the claim immediately loses its initial plausibility. For it has to be supposed that there are unlimited brain-states. There would have to be a possible highly specific brain-state to correlate with every specific intentional action which it could be conceivable to perform in chess, for example, even though one had never even heard of the game. And the same would apply to *every* other game and kind of activity which has been or could conceivably be devised. But more importantly, it can be seen that when proposed in terms of a correlation the claim does not in the least challenge or even touch my argument, and thus cannot constitute an objection. For whether or not anyone has a certain brain-state is quite irrelevant to our normal attributions of intention. If such a correlation were discovered it might in certain circumstances be useful *evidence* that someone did or did not have the relevant intention. But my point is that the discovery and confirmation of such a correlation would still depend upon the prior characterisation of the intention by reference to behavioural criteria. To illustrate this by means of an example, if someone whom I have offended takes every opportunity to chase me with a fiercely brandished hockey-stick, obviously intent on assault, my fears will not be assuaged by a scientist's assurance that, as a matter of fact, she does not have the requisite brain-state to intend me any harm.

To put the point another way, with respect to the members of another society it would still be necessary to characterise intentions, at least above a primitive level, in terms of *their* language and practices *before* any possible correlations could be determined. It is unintelligible to suppose the converse, namely that the brain-states could be determined first and independently.

In short, the only coherent explanation is in terms of an *internal*, logical connection between *behaviour*, including linguistic behaviour, and intentions. That is, intentions are characterised by their typical expression in overt behaviour. Just as the intention of the chess player cannot be given in terms of an *external*, stimulus-response kind of explanation but only in terms of the game, so the intentions involved in communication can be given only *internally*, in terms of a language.

We saw earlier that the ambiguity in the use of the term 'meaning' and its cognates may well contribute to misconceptions in empirical inquiry. For in one sense of the term, 'A means B' is equivalent to 'A is evidence of B', while in another sense it is equivalent to 'A logically entails, or is logically equivalent to, B'. Thus in the former sense one says 'Heavy oil consumption means a worn engine', and in the latter '"Bachelor" means "unmarried man"'. In the former sense, unlike the latter, the two entities or events are logically distinct. A closely related and perhaps more significant factor is that the very *nature* of scientific investigation contributes to this tendency towards dualism. For scientific investigation is concerned with the gathering of *evidence*, and therefore contingent rather than logical connections, and therefore with a dualistic approach. That is, evidence, and that for which it is evidence, are logically distinct. So there is likely to be a strong inclination for someone imbued with the methods of scientific investigation *always* to think of inquiry in dualistic terms, and therefore sometimes to apply such thinking to inappropriate situations. Specifically, he will tend to misconceive logical or conceptual relations, i.e. events which are internally related, in terms of evidential, contingent relations, i.e. events which are externally related and logically distinct. Thus, I suggest that it is precisely the way of thinking which is characteristic of scientific inquiry which tends to lead to the misconceptions we have been considering. Hence it is natural for Argyle to slide into exactly the same three forms of dualism which, in Chapter 8, we discovered to underlie and vitiate Eleanor Metheny's theory of meaning in movement. With respect to communication, he manifests the three dualistic misconceptions, each of which leads to incoherent subjectivism, in the following ways:

(1) He takes external behaviour as a *sign* of separately identifiable inner experiences and emotions (mind/body, or inner experience/overt behaviour, dualism).

(2) He regards language and works of art as *codes* carrying separately identifiable messages—he writes, for instance, of a 'correlation' between language and thought (meaning/medium of expression dualism).

(3) Partly because he conflates 'verbal' with 'linguistic', he has a

grossly oversimple conception of language as merely a code or *system of signals* which is distinct from, and constructed in order to send messages about, the real world. For example, he writes: 'Language is a very effective means of communicating information about physical objects, and public events in the *outside world*. It is good at describing and influencing behaviour. Language appears to have developed for these purposes . . .' (my italics) (language/reality dualism).

Now I hope it is abundantly clear that these criticisms of Argyle's work are not merely an exercise in verbal nit-picking with respect to the use of the term 'communication'. What I have tried to show is that there is an issue of considerable importance here, namely that it is a grave misconception to think that communication, in the sense I have characterised as lingcom, can coherently be explained by means of a causal, stimulus-response, evidential kind of investigation. Or, to put the point another way, if one wishes to use the term 'communication' in what I regard as the somewhat barbarous sense I characterised as percom, then it is a grave misconception to imagine that the communication which occurs in language can be coherently explained in the same way as non-linguistic behaviour. Initially I felt strongly inclined to express this point by saying baldly that an inquiry into communication, properly so-called, is a conceptual *not* an empirical matter. But that way of putting it is itself oversimple, and incurs the danger of another serious kind of misconception. It may be recalled that in Chapters 1 and 5 I characterised 'empirical' as 'going and seeing, the collecting of information etc.', as opposed to 'conceptual' which was characterised as 'considering the nature or meaning of the information one already has'. Thus it would be a fundamental mistake, and radically incompatible with my whole line of argument, to suggest that it would be unnecessary to 'go and see' where one wished to inquire into questions of communication. On the contrary, with respect, for instance, to an alien society I should want to insist that there could be no other way of establishing the relevant facts. The *only* way of finding out about the language and communication of the people in such a society would be by going there, joining them, immersing oneself in their culture and forms of behaviour. This is the only way in which one could understand their language, and thus the only way of being able to characterise the nature of their intentional actions, which, as we have seen, is necessary in order to recognise cases of communication. For it is *central* to my argument that an inquiry into communication cannot be *external*, but has to be *internal*, i.e. in terms of the language itself. It would be a serious misconception to imagine that such an inquiry could be conducted in terms of one's own, external language. Consequently, without a much sharper distinction between 'empirical' and 'conceptual' than I have yet encountered or been able to formulate myself, I cannot put the conclusion of the argument of this chapter in the bald statement that an inquiry into communication can coherently be conducted only in conceptual and not in empirical terms. Moreover, as will be clear from Chapter 5, there are causally necessary conditions for communication which are, of course, open to empirical investigation in the normal sense.

Nevertheless, it is clear that, in the sort of case envisaged, an inquiry into whether there was a language, and into questions of communication, would be completely different in kind from a scientific investigation of causes and causal reactions. As we have seen, communication depends upon the recognition of the character of intentional actions. The intention of a chess player can be characterised only internally, by reference to the rules and conventions of the game. No attempt at external explanation, by someone with no understanding of this or any relevantly similar game, could count as a characterisation of such an intention. Similarly, causal responses to the sounds uttered in an alien society could be determined *externally*, i.e. even if one did not understand the language, whereas to determine questions of meaning, of intentions, at least at anything above a very primitive level, and therefore of communication, it would be necessary to *learn* and understand the language and forms of life of the people in the society.

Wittgenstein (1953):

... in psychology there are experimental methods and conceptual *confusion* ... The existence of the experimental method makes us think we have the means of solving problems which trouble us; though the problem and method pass one another bv.

REFERENCES: CHAPTER 9

Argyle, M., *Bodily Communication* (London: Methuen, 1975).

Bennett, J. F., *Rationality* (London: Routledge & Kegan Paul, 1964).

Best, D., *Expression in Movement and the Arts* (London: Lepus Books, Henry Kimpton Publishers, 1974).

Bruce, V. R., *Dance and Dance Drama in Education* (Oxford: Pergamon Press, 1965).

Bruce, V. and Tooke, J., *Lord of the Dance* (Oxford: Pergamon Press, 1966).

Horst, L., 'Consider the question of communication', in *Anthology of Impulse 1951-1966*, ed. Marian Van Tuyl (New York City, New York: Impulse Publications, 1969).

Preston, V., *A Handbook for Modern Educational Dance* (London: Macdonald & Evans, 1963).

Shahn, B., *The Shape of Content* (Cambridge, Mass.: Harvard University Press, 1957).

Wittgenstein, L., *Philosophical Investigations* (Oxford: Basil Blackwell, 1953).

Wittgenstein, L., *Zettel* (Oxford: Basil Blackwell, 1967).

Index

Action also *see* Intention: intentional 32-3, 57-8, 74-83, 85, 94-8; voluntary 85; and moral responsibility 81-2; and movement 78-83; in context 78-83, 108-10, 136-7

Aesthetic: concept 101-3; content 99-100; experience 95-6, 113-22; judgment, reasons for 82; sports 103-10; and artistic 99, 113-22; and competitive 105; and psychology, *see* Psychology; and science 66-71, 75; as contemplative 111-12

Analytic philosophy 17

Answers 19-20

Argyle, M. 138, 140-1, 145, 150-61

Art: concept of 113-22; dance as, *see* Dance; sport as, *see* Sport; and communication 146-50

Artistic meaning 149, 153-5

Associative meaning 13, 126-31

Bambrough, J. R. 11, 29

Causes 74-8

Code, *see* Language

Communication 124, 128, 130-1, 138-61

Concepts 12-13, 123-4, 133-5, 151; quantification of 70

Conceptual: and empirical 65-87; and philosophical 65-6; and practical 60-2

Connotation 127-31

Context 79-83 *passim*, 93-8 *passim*, 108-12, 136-7, 149, 156-61

Dance: communication in 128, 146-50; definition of 90; empirical substantiation of 67-71, 90-1; meaning in 128-31, 146-50; movement 79-82; understanding of 147-50; as an art 30, 68-71, 115; as a universal language 149-50; as the basic or fundamental art 34-5

Definitions 19, 35, 40, 44, 88-90, 125

Dualism: body/mind 32-3, 53-4, 125-31, 159; language/reality 133-5, 159-60; meaning/medium of expression 131-2, 151-61

Empirical 9-11, 65-87, 129, 134, 150-61; methodology and the study of human movement 66-87, 88-98; and conceptual, *see* Conceptual

Epistemology 15, 53-4

Evidence and meaning 8-11, 140-1, 159

Experience of movement 33, 91-6, 110-12

Extended sense 42, 46-8

Eysenck, H. J. 72-4

Fact 83-5

Feeling, *see* Experience

Figure skating 120-1

Gymnastics 50-1, 104, 106; and dance 82, 113, 115

Human movement studies 50, 71, 85-7, 91-6, 97-8

Human kinetics 85-7

Idiosyncratic meaning 127-31

Imagination 85, 120

Independent, critical thought 5-6, 22-4

Inference 129-31

Infinite regress 57, 89

Inner experience, *see* Meaning, and Subjectivism

Intellect: as a general faculty 50-3; as an inner faculty 50, 53-4

Intelligence 52-3, 72-4

Intensional object 120

Intention: as a brain state 157-9; rationality, and language 138-61 *passim*; scientific analysis of 157-9

Intentional: action, *see* Action; communication 138-61 *passim*

Interpretation of dance 148-50

Intuition 80-1

Kinaesthetic: experience 93-6, 112; intellect 58-9

Laban, R. 27-37 *passim*

Language: and objectivity 13, 16-17, 123-37; and philosophy 14-17; and reality 14-17, 133-5, 159-60; or movement as a code 151-4, 159-60

Logical substantiation 10-11

164 / *Philosophy and Human Movement*

Meaning: naming theory of 53, 123-37 *passim*, 151-61 *passim*; and causal effects 76-8, 154-61; and medium of expression 13, 123-32 *passim*, 146-8, 151-61; and substantiation 8-11; as an inner idea 13, 124, 151-61; in dance, *see* Dance; in music 153-5; of action 75, 136-7

Means/end distinction 101-3

Metaphysics 15-17, 71, 80, 83

Metheny, Eleanor 51-2, 123-37, 159

Methodology in the study of human movement 91-8

Metric and non-metric rhythm 42-3

Motion 32-3

Movement: itself 88-98; and sense-perception 91-8; as a universal language 145-6

Non-verbal: arts 153-4; communication 138-61; expression 31-2, 138-61 *passim*

Objectivity 13, 16-17, 65-72, 80, 83, 94, 123-37; in artistic meaning 147-50; points of view 66-9, 96-7, 100

Observable criteria 93-8

Phenix, P. 55, 128-30

Phenomenology 68-9, 81, 88, 93, 94, 130

Philosophising 7

Philosophy: experiential 4; negative 21; of life 4-5; of sport and physical education 4, 17-22; second-order activity 6-8, 22; and language 9, 13-17

Physical movement 85

Practical performance and understanding 60-3

Psychology: and aesthetics 75-8; and communication 138-61 *passim*; and concept formation 62; and intelligence, *see* Intelligence

Purposive activities 101-10

Quantification 70-4, 90-3

Reasons and causes 36, 74-83, 154-61

Reid, L. A. 105, 111-12, 114-16

Ryle, G. 55, 62-3

Science: and the aesthetic 66-71; and logic 10-11; and objectivity 83-5, 94, 97; and philosophy 16-17, 28-9, 71-87 *passim*

Scientific: explanation 74-87 *passim*, 93, 97, 138, 150, 155-61; facts 83-5; and empirical 65-6

Signals 140-1, 152, 160

Signs 145-6

Sincerity and rationality 23-4

Spectator and performer 95-6, 110-12

Sport: and art 101, 113-22; as drama 117; as tragedy 117-19

Standard meaning 143-4

Stipulation 121, 143

Subjectivism 13, 81, 123-37 *passim*, 147-9, 151-61 *passim*

Symbolism 123-37

Titles of departments studying human movement 85-7

Thinking, feeling and doing 55-6, 58-9

Theory 83-5

Understanding 147-9

Value judgments 20-2

Verbal and linguistic 14-17, 138-46, 159-60

Winch, P. 15-16, 71-2

Wittgenstein, L. 5, 52, 54, 76, 81, 88, 95, 110, 125, 134, 141, 161

Words and language, *see* Verbal